MARSHMAN!

WILDLIFE EXPERIENCES OF

MANSON L. CLARK

OF COVE, TEXAS

■ ■ ■ ■ ■ ■

Kendon L. Clark

Marshman! Wildlife Experiences of Manson L. Clark of Cove, Texas
Extracted and Edited From His Journals by Kendon L. Clark

Please direct all correspondence and book orders to:
Kemp & Company
909 Harvard
Houston, Texas 77008
832.618.1416

First Printing
Yates Publishing Company
Ozark, Missouri
1983

Second Printing
Dogwood Printing Company
Ozark, Missouri
1989

Third Printing
Kemp & Company
Houston, Texas
2010

Published by Kemp & Company - Intelligent Solutions for Design & Print
Houston, Texas, 832.618.1416

Hard Cover: ISBN-13: 978-0-9822899-6-9 ISBN-10: 0-9822899-6-0
Soft Cover: ISBN-13: 978-0-9822899-5-2 ISBN-10: 0-9822899-5-2

TABLE OF CONTENTS

▪ PREFACE ▪

Historians throughout the ages have speculated – even dreamed – as to how the field of history would profit if every human being took the time and effort to record in writing the events of his or her life, regardless of how minor they might appear to the individual in the worldwide scheme of time. After all, history is nothing more than the collective record of mankind, his dreams, achievements and failures. While many great political, military and civil leaders have recorded their memoirs, and even auto-biographies for posterity, the number of these is far less than historians would like. But, for the common man, the individual whose life is rarely known to many people outside his local sphere of endeavor, few such records exist, much to the chagrin of those who would attempt to compile histories of local areas and regions.

Manson Lee Clark of the rural Chambers County, Texas community of Cove compiled such a record, spanning more than sixty years of his outdoor experiences and observations with the wildlife of southeast Texas. In all truthfulness, it must be stated that Clark did not have the future work of historians in mind when he began keeping records so many years ago. He simply recorded facts, figures and dates for his own future reference, rather than having to face the prospect of later relying upon his memory to recall such matters. The result became the compilation of probably one of the most detailed accounts of outdoor life in south-east Texas during the better part of the twentieth century. It consists of all the ingredients of man's endeavors: achievements, failures, trials and errors. It records from an individual perspective both the good and difficult times.

The author of the original sets of notes and journals from which this study is taken paid little heed to description or explanation. Rather, he wrote with the forthright manner that comes from years and decades of knowledge in his chosen field of endeavor. Such style caused this editor to make repeated trips to the subject's home to ask, "When did this take place?" or "Where did that happen?", the result being that the bulk of this book is largely written in the words of the editor while based entirely upon the subject's writings.

The ancestral lineage of Manson Clark, consuming much of the first chapter, was researched and written by the editor as little such material appeared in the original notes of the subject.

Chapter 9 of this study comes under the title of "The Marshman's Journal" and is exactly that. It is a collection from the notes and journals of the subject and is reproduced here in almost exact original form. Only very minor editing has been allowed to enter this section of the work, and then only to clarify some points which might not be readily understandable to the novice or casual reader. It is this chapter which embodies the real expression of the Marshman! It would have perhaps been preferable that the entire manuscript of this work appear in this form, although the editor deemed such inadvisable as numerous details of many events would have been left to the discretion of the reader.

Some occurrences have been purposely deleted. The writer of the original journals, the subject of this sketch, insisted that nothing go into print which might cast others in a humorous or disfavorable manner. Other points of legal nature have also been omitted due to the impossibility of acquiring certain documentation without which the printing of such material might have stood on shaky legal grounds.

For all practical purposes, this little volume covers the history of an entire era, at least as the era has pertained to the subject himself. There are few who would dare to speculate that the hunting, trapping and fishing will ever again be as it has been during the era herein related. It would be understandable if Manson Clark appeared bitter about the things which he observed in the once tranquil marshlands of Cove. But, although he admitted in these pages his deep yearning that things could once again be as they were in the marshes, he was too much of a realist to allow himself to think it could happen. His lack of bitterness might be explained in the fact that he realized he had lived through a better time and enjoyed the fruits of the Creator. He was aware that succeeding generations would not know of the "Golden Age" of the southeast Texas marshlands, except for the knowledge they might glean from books and other reminiscences. But, he had been there and considered himself fortunate to have experienced what others in the future can only read about.

Kendon L. Clark
Cove, Texas
January 1983
Revised November 2010

▪ PROFILE OF THE SUBJECT OF THIS SKETCH ▪

NAME: Manson Lee Clark

BIRTH: November 28, 1905, at Cove, Texas

PARENTS: William Daniel & Florence (Smith) Clark

DEATH: August 6, 1986, at Cove, Texas

BURIAL: Clark Family Cemetery, Cove, Texas

SEX & RACE: Male / Caucasian

HEIGHT & WEIGHT: 6 Ft. / 200 Lbs.

COLOR OF HAIR & EYES: Black / Brown

RELIGION: Church of Christ

FRATERNAL AFFILIATION: Hood's Texas Brigade Association

MARRIAGES: (1) Cormelia Mildred Fannett
                                   (2) Elmyra Ester Maley

CHILDREN   (1) Gloria Gertrude Clark
                                   (2) Freda Marie Clark
                                   (3) Florrie Gene Clark (deceased)
                                   (4) Kendon Lee Clark

PATERNAL LINE OF ANCESTRY: Manson Lee Clark, William Daniel Clark,
                                   Barton Clark, William Clark,
                                   Carpus Clark, Eleazer Clark,
                                   Benoni Clark, William Clark, Jr.,
                                   William Clark, Sr. (Immigrant)

MATERNAL LINE OF ANCESTRY: Manson Lee Clark, Florence Smith,
                                   John Smith, Silas Smith,
                                   Jesse Smith (Immigrant Unknown)

▪ CHAPTER I ▪

ANCESTRY AND CHILDHOOD

Both the paternal and maternal ancestry of Manson Clark hint of the restless pioneer spirit of the early American frontiersmen. Their journeys through the wilderness regions of America during the first two and a half centuries of American settlement culminated in the new frontier of Texas during the first half century of the 1800's. Texas would be their final challenge, their permanent home, and the end of westward expansion for the ancestors of the subject of this sketch.

▪ ▪ ▪ ▪ ▪ ▪

The paternal side of Clark's ancestry has its American roots deep in New England. Lieutenant William Clark was born at Plymouth, Devonshire, England in 1609, and took passage for the "New World" in 1633 aboard the "Mary and John." Settling first at Dorchester, Massachusetts, he took a wife named Sarah in 1637, and they had ten children, all born at Dorchester. In 1659, the family removed to Northampton, Massachusetts. There, the immigrant Clark served as selectman, court deputy, and associate judge, and was one of the founders of the settlement's first church. He served in the Royal military service against the Indians during King Philip's War.

The ninth child of William and Sarah Clark was William Clark, Jr., born July 3, 1656. William, Jr. married Rebecca Cooper of Springfield, but following the birth of their first child, Rebecca died in 1678. He remarried in 1680 to Hannah Strong, daughter of Elder John Strong of the prolific Strong family of Massachusetts. William Clark, Jr. became a captain of militia and served as a governmental representative from Northampton for four years. He bought a large tract of land from the Mohegan Indians which came to be known as the "Clark and Dewey Purchase." William and Hannah Clark had seven children, all probably born at Northampton. He died on September 3, 1704.

The seventh child of William, Jr. and Hannah Clark was a son named Benoni, so styled from the old biblical name meaning "child of my sorrow and pain" (Genesis 35:16-20) as his mother died within days after his birth. Born January 31, 1694, he moved with his family in 1700 to Lebanon, Connecticut where, in 1718, he married one Hannah Root, daughter of Thomas Root, one of the founders of Hartford, Connecticut. Benoni engaged as a farmer and he and his wife had twelve children within a period of some twenty years. The third child born to this union was a son named Eleazer.

Eleazer Clark was born to Benoni and Hannah Clark at Lebanon, Connecticut, August 25, 1724. He was married at Lebanon on April 25, 1747 to Miss Esther Gibbs, daughter of John and Sarah Gibbs of Claremont, New Hampshire. Eleazer and Esther Clark had ten children, all born at Lebanon.

The ninth child, a son, of Eleazer and Esther Clark was Corpus (sometimes spelled "Carpus"), born February 3, 1768. In 1792, Corpus Clark married Miss Phoebe Green, the marriage taking place at Claremont, New Hampshire. Corpus and Phoebe must have moved westward into the sparsely populated region of central Vermont soon after their marriage, because their first child, Guy, was born at Weathersfield, Vermont in 1793. Land records indicate that Corpus Clark owned property in Washington County, Vermont at least as early as 1802. He soon became involved in Vermont politics. From 1806 to 1810, he served as town clerk of Worcester, and as town representative from 1809 to 1811, and again in 1813. He appears in the records as a Washington County justice of the peace in 1811, road commissioner in 1812, and as 1st constable in 1813. During the latter year, Corpus Clark was living in Rutland County from which he was elected to the Vermont Legislature. In his tenure there, the people of the State had failed to elect a new governor and the decision was thereby thrown into the Legislature. It became the most hotly debated issue for the governing body in many years, and Corpus Clark was one of those who rose to the floor and soundly castigated the nominee of an opposing faction, adding that if the Legislature chose the wrong man as governor, Vermont would no longer be a fit place to live. The "wrong man" was elected, at least in the view of Corpus, and he wasted no time in making his word good. According to the Vermont Historical Gazetteer, in an article written in 1868, Corpus "did so remove, immediately after the rising of the Legislature," taking with him his family and items of "prosperity–a span of fine horses, etc." This occurrence took place during the same year, 1813, in which his eldest son, Guy, died from wounds received in the War of 1812.

Between 1814 and 1820, perhaps the entire family journeyed down the Ohio River, settling for a few years at Ironton, Lawrence County, Ohio. Here, at least two of the sons of Corpus were married, Barton being wed to Hannah Hanley. William, second youngest of Corpus' sons and the great-grandfather of Manson Clark, having been born in Vermont on November 27, 1803, married Miss Louisa Jane Callihan at Ironton, on August 5, 1824. Corpus' wife, Phoebe, died September 9, 1823, probably in Lawrence County, Ohio.

Between 1825 and '30, the sons of Corpus Clark, Barton, William and the youngest, Daniel, began working their way farther down the Ohio River to its confluence with the Mississippi. Their trek to Texas had finally begun.

The first mention we find of the Clark family entering Texas is the "Certificate of Entrance" of Barton Clark at Nacogdoches, dated April 2, 1835. Before the end of the year, Barton and William had arrived in the Houston County, Texas area. The aging Corpus would join them there in 1839, and he, Barton and William would each acquire land grants from the newly established Republic of Texas, located near the east bank of the Trinity River in southwestern Houston County. Corpus Clark died on January 8, 1840, and was buried in the soil of east Texas, many hundreds of miles from his native Lebanon, Connecticut.

In Houston County, the Clark brothers prospered. Barton became an extensive property holder, with cattle and slaves. Younger brother Daniel became a husband, marrying Miss Mary Morse on October 10, 1837.

William, the middle brother, in terms of chronological birth, had married Miss Louisa Jane Callihan in Ironton, Ohio, as we have already noted. During their slow trek to Texas, they had at least two children (perhaps more were born. but only two had survived to arrive in Texas with their parents). Soon after their arrival in Texas, their third child, a son whom they named Barton was born. Named for his uncle, the elder Barton, this given name was now beginning to take hold among the family and would be continued for several generations.

William Clark was appointed, in 1841, by the Republic of Texas as a trustee to the planned Trinity College to be erected in Houston County. The death date of William Clark has not survived the tests of time, but must have come by 1850, as all records of his name in the region disappear at that time.

William's death left his widow, Louisa Jane, to care for their three children, Nancy Louisa, Josephine and Barton. In about 1850, Louisa Jane and her children joined her brother-in-law, Daniel, and his family in removing southward down the Trinity River into southern Liberty County (that portion which in 1858 would become Chambers County), at the head of Trinity Bay. Daniel and his family settled at Wallisville on the east side of the river, as did the widow, Louisa Jane. The widow Clark's eldest daughter, Nancy Louisa, had married one Robert Kilgore before leaving Houston County and they likewise settled in the Wallisville area. The younger daughter, Josephine, married Robert W. Lawrence, son of pioneer settler, Joseph Lawrence, in 1853, and they settled down to family life on Lawrence's Island, just west of the mouth of the Trinity River. Young Barton spent the remainder of his boyhood days with Robert and Josephine on Lawrence's Island, adopting the life of a hunter and fisherman as only a young man in such an environment is capable.

In late 1860, Barton Clark left Lawrence's Island and moved to the mainland of the Cove community, on the A.B.J. Winfree Survey, where he built a small cabin on the east bank of Cotton Bayou. His nearest neighbors were the Algiers family who lived just down the bayou, some one half mile distant. He must have become fast friends with William and Samuel Algiers, young men near his own age. With the secession of Texas from the Union in early 1861, and its joining the Confederate States of America, the young men volunteered their services to fight for the South in the Confederate armed forces. Barton Clark and William Algiers joined the infantry unit known as the Bayland Guards, which soon became Company C of the Second Texas Infantry Regiment. Samuel Algiers joined the horsemen of Spaights Texas Cavalry Battalion.

Barton came home on furlough from the army in early 1862, and used the occasion to marry Miss Narcissa Henrietta Ophelia Jane Barrow, daughter of west Trinity Bay pioneer Solomon Barrow. Soon returning to military service, he contracted a disease diagnosed by army doctors as pthysis, or pulmonary tuberculosis. Considered to be terminally ill, Private Clark was sent home to die. After he returned home from the service, Henrietta gave birth to their daughter, Martha Emily, who became known as "Mattie", on March 18, 1863. Two sons would later be born to Barton and Henrietta. William Daniel Clark, father of the subject of this sketch was born July 9, 1864, and Barton Daniel, September 8, 1866. All three children were born on the Solomon Barrow property at West Bay, where the Clark family had made their home. Finally, in 1868, Barton Clark lost his battle with the incurable disease and died at age 28. He was buried near the old Solomon Barrow home site.

Widowed now with three young children, the oldest of whom was only five years of age, Henrietta married one Solomon Curbello. This marriage, however, was doomed to failure and lasted only some two months. In 1870, she was wooed into matrimony by Benjamin W. Tilton, himself a Confederate veteran as had been her first two husbands. In taking Henrietta as his wife, Tilton also accepted her three Clark children and bestowed as much love upon them as if they had been his own. All three of the Clark children reached adulthood. Mattie married James Monroe Robinson and they settled north of the old Barrow property and had twelve children. Barton Daniel married Sarah Fisher and also settled at West Bay.

William Daniel Clark crossed the Trinity River to the central part of Chambers County to find his bride near the banks of Double Bayou. She was Miss Florence Smith, daughter of John and Celestine Smith of Double Bayou.

■ ■ ■ ■ ■ ■ ■

The earliest proven ancestor on the maternal side of the genealogy of Manson Clark was one Silas Smith, born about 1782 in South Carolina. There are indications that his parents might have been a couple known as Jesse and Sarah Ann Smith, but lineal connection to this union remains uncertain.

Silas Smith is believed by some to have come to southeast Texas as early as 1819, and perhaps established a cabin home soon thereafter. He was in Louisiana during the mid-1820's, however, where on September 11, 1827, he married Mrs. Lurinda (Green) Wilburn, widow of Elijah Wilburn. Lurinda was a native of the State of Georgia, having been born there about 1792.

Silas and Lurinda Smith had four children: Calvin, Silas Jr., John and Lurinda. John Smith, the third child, was born near Hankamer in Liberty County (later north central Chambers County) on January 10, 1832.

In 1861, John Smith enlisted in the Confederate States Army. He has been variously listed as having served in Company F, Fifth Texas Infantry Regiment of the famed Hood's Texas Brigade, as well as with the First Texas Heavy Artillery and a cavalry battalion. In early 1863, Private Smith came home on a furlough and married Miss Celestine Fruge', the marriage taking place at Liberty, county seat of Liberty County.

John and Celestine Smith had six children who lived to maturity: Malina, Silas (III), Edward, Florence (mother of the subject of this sketch), Manson Kirby, and Wilburn Lloyd. Miss Florence Smith, the fourth of those listed above, was born September 17, 1872, at Double Bayou, Texas.

■ ■ ■ ■ ■ ■ ■

William Daniel Clark and Florence Smith were married at the home of Benjamin and Henrietta Tilton in Cove, Texas on April 16, 1890. At the time of their marriage, William was twenty-five years of age and his bride, seventeen. The first four years of their marriage were spent on the John Smith property near Double Bayou. On August

17, 1893, William purchased sixty-seven and one-half acres of land from Dr. G. H. D. Fielden for a total of $135.00, at a rate of $2.00 per acre. The property was located on the A.B.J. Winfree Survey in Cove, north of Cotton Lake. Its eastern boundary was the center of Spring Branch Gully from which point it extended westward for almost a mile along the northern boundary of the William Maley property.

When William and Florence Clark removed from Double Bayou to Cove, they had already had two children. The first, John Milton, had been born in November 1891, but had lived only a few days. The second child was a daughter, Pansy Augusta, born August 6, 1893, and died in Houston, August 31, 1973. After moving to Cove, six more children were born into the household, all born at Cove, during the next twelve years: Elsie Celestine, born October 3, 1897, died August 25, 1977 in Houston; William Edward, born October 18, 1900, died March 15, 1972 in Dayton; Martha Verie, born August 9, 1903, died October 12,1986 in Houston; Manson Lee (subject of this study), born November 28, 1905, died August 6, 1986 at Cove; Henrietta Lillian, born January 28, 1907, died February 14, 1907 at Cove; and, Vane Barton, born September 4, 1909, died December 23,1989 at Cove.

William Clark built a two-story house near the eastern end of his property just up the rise in the land from Spring Branch Gully. He took up the usual profession of the region in the planting of cotton, although he diversified his crop on some of his acreage in the planting of an annual onion crop. He also planted an orchard of several varieties of fruit trees in the fertile soil between his house and the west bank of the gully. The usual assortment of cows to provide for milk for the family and horses and mules to pull the farm implements necessitated the inclusion of barns and pens near the house, as well as storage buildings for onions and grain.

When Manson Lee Clark was born in the farm home at Cove on November 28, 1905, his childhood work was already cut out for him, as indeed it was for his brothers and sisters. A family farm was exactly that; it took a family to hold it together and make it productive.

■ ■ ■ ■ ■ ■ ■

Some of Manson's earliest memories of his childhood in Cove were fond ones, occurring before he was old enough to take much of an active role in the work of the farm. At the age of three or four years, he would make his way on foot through the woods north of Cotton Lake to a natural terrain feature known locally as Hugo Point where lived

Mrs. Metta Wilburn, approximately a mile from the Clark home. Known as "Trick" to most local residents, she was a daughter of pioneer settler Hugo Franssen, Sr. The Franssen family had settled on the Point during the early 1850's, and raised a large family. The elder family members having died years earlier and the other brothers and sisters having taken up abode elsewhere, primarily in the Old River community north of Cove, Trick and her husband, Milton Wilburn, were now the only residents on Hugo Point, a location which offered a beautiful view of both Cotton Lake and Old River Lake and the surrounding marshlands.

Trick won the heart of the little country boy by showing him a great deal of attention whenever he came to visit. She knew, however, that his real motive for walking through the woods to her home was one in the form of a tasty delicacy she always served him upon his visits. In later years, Manson recalled that Trick Wilburn had the best syrup, butter and bread in Cove. The syrup was made at the Wilburn syrup mill near a dry gully just west of Hugo Point and the butter was churned right there on the Point. Trick also made her own bread, as such was the primary method of the time for the procurement of the commodity. His taste for syrup, butter and bread would be one to last throughout his life. Trick Wilburn died in 1909 from an overdose of headache medicine. Manson would be a grown man before he would ever realize just who this lady was who had always been so ready to bestow her attention on a little boy from across the woods. The only name he had ever known her by had been "Trick.".

There was a time not too many decades ago when the federal government had not yet taken it upon itself to cure the ills of the whole world or even to become the caretaker of the indigent population within its own borders. In such times, widows, orphans and the disabled were cared for on a local basis and it was the responsibility of local or county governments to locate caring citizens willing to see to the needs of the less fortunate. In such cases, the county would usually pay the caretaker a sum within the range of $10 to $20 per month for such care of an invalid.

Mrs. Annie Guinea, a widow who had been born in Germany in 1833, presented such a case in Cove. She and her husband, who was a native of France, had come to America in about 1865. She was childless and once explained her lack of children in her broken English with its German accent: "I did tried, and Guinea, he did tried," yet no offspring had been forthcoming. Therefore, with the death of her husband and old age creeping upon her, rendering her incapable of caring for herself, and with no other family members to see to her needs, she was forced to "go on the county," as the terminology was in that day. Dr. Solomon Williams had originally taken on the care for Mrs. Guinea, but upon his death in December 1909, the widow was again without anyone to care for her. Moved by her desperate situation, William Clark contracted with the county to take on her care following the death of Dr. Williams.

Clark built Mrs. Guinea a one-room house on his property just east of where his family's house stood. Four-year-old Manson, while already doing some work in the fields with his older brothers and sisters, but probably unable yet to keep up with his elders along the seemingly endless cotton rows, was given the duty of carrying Mrs. Guinea's food to her at meal times after it had been prepared by his mother, Florence, in the main house.

Once the family heard a commotion inside Mrs. Guinea's house and family members ran to see what had happened. William had caught a striped-head turtle that day and brought it to Mrs. Guinea as he knew turtle meat to be one of her favorite foods. She had said she would butcher the reptile herself if Florence would cook it for supper. The offer was accepted. In the usual manner of accomplishing the task, she had cut the hard shell from the turtle and placed all the entrails into the upside-down natural receptacle, then set the entire mess on the floor beside her bed. Doubtlessly, absent-minded in her current physical condition, she had neglected to take the shell and entrails outside before retiring to bed early that night. Soon after falling asleep, she had been disturbed by a nightmare and rolled out of her bed onto the floor. Her head went directly into the turtle shell, the appendages on either side of the shell securely locking themselves into the temples of her head. When her caretakers arrived at her door, she had risen from the floor, the turtle shell still firmly clasped and the entrails therein hanging about her face and neck. Such a sight, while perhaps comical at first glance, caused young Manson to feel a deep sense of pity for this good woman who had thus been so degraded by her physical condition.

On another occasion, when some four or five years of age, Manson was going about the familiar task of carrying Mrs. Guinea's meal to her from the main house. Unaware that a swarm of bees had taken over the little house, he entered with the platter of food and, amid the incessant buzzing of the insects, set the container on a small table near Mrs. Guinea's bedside. Just as he noticed that the elderly woman was still in bed with her mosquito bar netting firmly affixed about her for protection, the bees covered him and inflicted their painful stings on every exposed part of his anatomy. Running outside, Manson headed for the Clark house, the disturbed bees trailing along behind him, dashing additional stings into the boy with every few steps. Put to bed with a fever of almost 105 degrees, it was several days before his condition was nursed back within normal range and he was able to resume his normal childhood activities.

Another encounter with hostile insects a couple years later left an impression on the young boy he would never forget. At about six years of age, Manson was fond of climbing the pear trees in the family orchard to pick a couple of the ripe, juicy specimens and then sit on the ground at the base of the tree to enjoy the tasty fruits of his labor. On one such occasion while ascending one of the pear trees, he had failed to notice a nest of yellow jackets hanging from a limb directly above him. As he scrambled toward a higher limb in quest of an especially large pear, the insects became disturbed and "bristled up" by the shaking of the tree during his ascent. With his view locked on the pear, the object of his struggle, he unintentionally thrust his head directly into the yellow jacket nest. By a later count of the stings, exactly thirteen of the yellow jackets got into his hair, mercilessly stinging the boy all over his scalp. The sudden shock of the great number of stings to his head knocked Manson loose from the tree limbs and rendered him unconscious by the time he struck the ground. He had no idea as to how long he lay beneath the tree before being found by other members of the family who nursed him back to his senses.

With his increase in age, so came an increase in his responsibilities on the family farm. Long days were spent in chopping and picking cotton, rounding up the horses and mules for the day's work, and – the job Manson hated worse than all others – cutting onions in the onion barn. The family onion crop was an important supplement to the family's cotton income each year. After harvest, the onions were stored in an onion barn, or "crib," to be held until the market was at a point to make their sale profitable for the farm. The onions could not be allowed to merely lay in the crib in a dormant and undisturbed state during the interim. At least once per week they had to be sorted through, and those which begun showing too much of an inclination toward rotting had to be culled out and thrown away. Others which had developed small dark spots on them had to be manually cut to remove such impurities. It was a necessary job on the farm, but importance did little to impress Manson as he and his brothers and sisters spent endless days with tearful eyes inside the onion crib. This experience would have a lasting effect on Manson as even in advanced age, he preferred to have his meals cooked without the use of onions as a natural additive.

At about age seven or eight, Manson began helping his older brother, Bill (William Edward), to catch the horses and mules in the early morning for the elder William's use during the day of plowing in the fields. It seemed that every morning the work animals, as well as the cows which had to be rounded up for the morning milking routine, were to be found at the far western end of the Clark property, which was almost a mile in length. It was the job of the boys to walk to the far end of the property and drive the animals back to the barn lot where the horses and mules were to be harnessed and the cows coaxed into giving some amount of milk for the use of the family.

The ten cows on the property did not give too much trouble during the daily routine, perhaps because they had learned that their morning ordeal would be of brief duration and they would soon be released back into the pasture to resume their grazing. The horses were the real devils of the pack. They seemed to possess the mental ability to thwart the best intentions of man and certainly had the agility and speed to support their own intentions. As often as not, it seemed, the horses would allow the boys to drive them almost to the barn area, where they nervously congregated together (Manson always believed they were planning their next move), then suddenly make a wild bolt around the boys and head back toward the far end of the pasture, their heads held high in their gallop as if laughing at their temporary victory over Bill and Manson. On such occasions, there was nothing else to do but walk again to the far end of the property and again begin the process of rounding up the animals for another trip toward the barn lot. Bill and Manson truly believed that the horses were intelligent enough to plan their devious means of escape and that when they gathered together prior to their lightning run back down in the pasture, they were actually "talking" to each other quietly as to how to go about shirking their day's work in the harnesses. At an early age, Manson pledged to himself that if he ever was able to get away from farming when he reached manhood, he would never again own a horse, mule or cow.

As on most rural farms, William Clark's horses were kept strictly for the purpose of working the fields or to pull a buggy or wagon when the family made an occasional trip to visit friends or relatives some distance away, such as at Barbers Hill or West Bay. It was practically unheard of, however, to use one of the valuable animals for such frivolity as pleasure-riding or short excursions within the confines of Cove itself. William did have an aging gray mare, however, which he rarely used any longer for working the fields, and had pretty well retired her to the pasture for her old age. It must have seemed like a real luxury when William began allowing Manson to use the old mare to ride to Joseph's Store, on the shore of Old River Lake, to retrieve the family mail or purchase a few items of necessity not grown on the farm. But it did not take long for Manson to learn that even this aging specimen of horseflesh had a peculiarity which he considered much less than desirable. The old mare always did fine as he rode her from home to the store. Arriving at his destination, he would tie the bridle reins to the hitching rack before the establishment and go inside to take care of his father's business. When he emerged from the building, the sight which greeted him was always the same: an empty bridle dangling by the reins tied to the rack. The old mare never failed to pull her head out of the bridle while Manson was busy inside the store, and turn and head for home, leaving the boy to walk the two miles back to the farm, carrying the mail and commodities, as well as the bridle. This repeated process did little to improve Manson's estimation of domesticated farm animals.

One day in about 1910 or '11, Manson and some of the other Clark children were out in the yard when they began to smell something quite alien to their senses. As the odor grew stronger, it developed an accompanying sound, likewise unfamiliar, coming up the dusty trail to their home. The smell turned out to be that of gasoline and the noise was coming from an automobile, a Model "T" Ford car to be exact. Its driver was Uncle Manson Smith, a brother to Florence (Smith) Clark and the man after whom young Manson had been named. Uncle Manson had just bought the newfangled contraption and had come all the way from Double Bayou to show it off to his Cove kinfolks. This being the first car the family had seen (no one in Cove owned one as yet), everyone gathered around the vehicle, admiring its sleek, shiny finish. Uncle Manson gave a "honk" on the squeeze-bulb horn and almost sent the kids into panic. Eager to demonstrate to his relatives this new innovation of modern technology, he offered to take the family for a ride. He did not have to make his offer more than once as the family began climbing into the vehicle, hanging onto everything that would provide a hand hold. Away they went through Cove, passing an occasional house from which the occupants would emerge to find out what the source of that odor and noise might be. The machine rattled its way to the Old River Lake ferry, operated by the sons of the late Dr. Solomon Williams, and floated to the east side of the lake on the conveyance. The ferry operator that day would really have something to tell the family when he got home that night! Traveling along on the ridge between Lost River and Trinity River, Uncle Manson held tightly to the steering wheel and opened the throttle all the way. Glancing back at his nephew, Manson, seated directly behind the driver's chair, the elder man cautioned, "Hang on, honey! We're doin' thirty miles an hour!" Later, when safely back at their Cove home, William Clark determined that he, too, would purchase an automobile for his family. He would realize that intention in the not too distant future.

In 1914, Manson Clark began formal education at the age of eight years. The Cove school was located near the west shore of Old River Lake in the vicinity of a small tributary locally known as Merritt Gully. This small area, not more than a half mile square, had become somewhat of the commercial center of Cove, if indeed any part of Cove could be thusly called. Here was located the general merchandise stores of Charles T. Joseph, Sr. and Daniel M. Icet, and in later years Alvin Fisher would open yet a third such business establishment for the service of the people of Cove. The Cove post office was housed inside the Joseph Store and Dr. Solomon Williams had also conducted his medical profession nearby at his home at the mouth of the gully. In addition to the education of young minds, church services were also held at the school building. The ferry landing on the Cove side of the lake was located a short distance south of Merritt Gully, and several home sites were occupied in the little area by the families of Eli Hill, Llewellyn White, Charley and Hugh Welch, and Allen Voortman. On any map of Chambers County with plotted points indicating the locations of the county's numerous small communities, it was this area which would be used to pinpoint the settlement of Cove.

Manson and his brothers and sisters had approximately a mile and a half to walk to school from their farm home near Spring Branch Gully. The usual route was through the woods along the gully, northeastward through the pastures of David Harmon and Waelder McKay, often walking the distance in the company of the children of the Maley and Wilburn families who also resided in the lower Cove area. The old adage so often related to children by members of an earlier generation about walking to school barefoot in all kinds of weather was more than just an old wives tale to these children. Shoes were not always easy to come by in Cove at that time and when a pair was owned, no one wanted to wear them out in the daily drudgery of school attendance.

Manson soon found an excuse to begin veering from the usual route to school each morning. It was a time of great population of skunks, or polecats, in the Cove woods. Learning that a few dollars could be realized from the sale of the furs of the animals, Manson borrowed a few old rusty steel traps his father kept hanging on a wall inside the barn which were used only occasionally to control predators around the family chicken pen. Manson believed he had found an even better use for the traps than predator control and began setting a few of them in likely places in the woods and along the gully banks for the odor-bearing creatures. As he continued to add more traps to his trap line, strung out in a general direction toward the school house, his route to the daily toil of book learning varied more and more each day as he walked from trap to trap en route to school.

One morning as he approached a trap in which lay a polecat, the animal immediately prepared for battle before Manson could apply a killing blow to the head of the trapped creature. In the skunk's notorious manner of waging warfare against both man and beast, the tail of the animal was raised and the boy caught the full blast of the musk all over his body. Temporarily deterred from his task, Manson nevertheless went ahead and took his prey. Checking the rest of his trap line on the way to school, he entered the classroom just at the beginning of class time. When he walked into the room, heads were raised and noses twitched. The teacher, Miss Robbie Montgomery, looked at Manson, turned up her nose, and made a grimace not unlike that of a smashed frog. Unwilling to have her class, or her nasal senses, disrupted for the entire day by the strong perfume-odor emanating from Manson's otherwise clean clothes, the teacher sent him home for the day. Nothing could have suited Manson better. Home he went at a faster rate than he usually employed in traveling to school. Hurriedly separating the skin from the animal he had caught that morning, he took a few more traps from the barn and headed back into the woods to make more sets. His mother worked with every tactic she knew to cleanse his clothes that day of the offensive stench, but nothing was found to accomplish the job. Finally, the clothes were buried to rid the home of the lingering smell.

On another occasion while running his school-route trap line, Manson had an even more dispiriting experience with another skunk which he found ready to do battle. Checking a trapset at the head of a dry gully a short distance from his home, the boy found that something had stepped into the trap and had crawled into an armadillo hole located a few inches from where he had made the set. All that was visible of the set was the trap stake, which securely anchored the trap to the ground, and the chain connecting the trap to the stake. The chain trailed from the stake into the darkness of the small tunnel. Eager to learn what was in the trap on the hidden end of the chain, Manson took hold of the steel links and began tugging in an effort to extract the trapped animal out of the hole. The polecat was caught by a rear foot and as the animal began to emerge from the armadillo hole, the sight should have made the boy shudder as he recalled in an instant what had happened to him not long ago, the reason for which he was sent home from school.

The sight that greeted him on this occasion was the familiar upraised black and white tail – the south end of a northbound skunk. Instantly, Manson's mouth dropped open as he tried to determine what to do, but he would not release his hold on the trap chain. Suddenly, that same terrible stench again made contact with him, this time directly in his face and more specifically, into his gaping mouth. Jarred by the turn of events, Manson was now quick to drop the chain and allow the animal to again retreat to the safety of the hole. The boy coughed and gagged in vain attempts to rid his mouth and throat of the sickening musk. Determined to return later and secure the fur of the animal for which he had paid dearly, he was not up to the task at this moment. Racing for the open well in the Clark yard, he drank and spat out what seemed to be an entire bucketful of water, but the fumes remained. Suddenly feeling sick to his stomach, Manson went inside the house and, speaking around coughs and gasps, told his concerned mother what had happened to him. Sympathetic as sometimes only a mother can be in such cases, Florence must have wondered if this experience might dampen the desire in her son to deal so directly with wildlife. Indeed, if Manson was ever to be deterred in what was rapidly becoming a sought after way of life for him, this experience should have served as that deterrent.

Manson and his older brother, Bill, began teaming up to trap coons, possums and rabbits in the woods. In later years, Manson would often state that Bill was probably the best coon trapper in these parts. Bill had a recipe for concocting a special liquid bait for the masked animals, an enticement which "no coon in his right mind could resist." The bait, a combination of several portions of various animal entrails, waste and even household refuse, was mixed together in a jar, tightly sealed, and buried for a long period of time. The longer the concoction was buried, the more irresistible it supposedly was to the coon. Only a few drops of the bait were usually needed to attract the animal to the vicinity of the trap. It was applied with an eye dropper to a tree truck or bush near the trap. Being in liquid form, the bait soaked into the bark and became practically invisible. Upon being drawn to the area of the scent, the coon would usually walk around the location several times in search of the source of the smell. With his attention drawn exclusively to the odor, he would usually disregard all caution and inevitably step into the trap, securely fastened at ground level and lightly covered with leaves and dust.

In later years, Manson would recall an old coon he and his friend Ed Hill once found inside a hollow log which had been lying on the ground for years and was now in a semi-rotten condition. They both had firearms, but determined to try to catch the coon without shooting him in order to ensure a better condition of his hide. They set eleven traps in a small cluster on the ground directly in front of one end of the log. Then, they went around to the other end with some sticks or fallen limbs and began to tease the coon, hoping to drive him out of the log and into the traps. They reasoned that it was impossible for the animal to exit the far end of the log unscathed by the array of steel in his path.

Finally, the old coon had enough of their play and headed out the end of the log, just as Manson and Ed had planned. The boys stood silently as the furry creature emerged from the hollow, looked around slowly at the uncovered traps clustered on the ground before him, and stepped into the trap field. Taking his time, the coon gingerly stepped between each of the traps, being careful not to touch any of them in his treacherous stroll. Upon clearing the last of the traps, the coon suddenly bolted away from the area and disappeared into the woods beyond. Manson and Ed, observing the entire affair, stood dumbfounded and unable to completely comprehend what they had just seen. Only then did the boys realize that their firearms were near at hand and they could have easily secured them and killed the coon rather than allowing him to merely amble away as they stood looking on. But, they had to admit that any animal which was that intelligent deserved to live. That thought somewhat assuaged their otherwise crumpled feelings as they began removing the traps from before the log, a cluster of steel which only a few minutes before they were certain was going to bag them a big coon.

While a few cottontail rabbits were found in the prairie regions of Cove, the woods and gully areas were populated primarily by the larger swamp rabbits. It seemed next to impossible to effectively catch many of the rabbits in the common steel leg hold traps due to the rodents' manner of leaping while on the move, making the chances of a rabbit's foot landing in a trap very slim at best. Therefore, Bill had begun constructing wooden "live traps" whereby the small animal would often go into the man-made tunnel as if he were entering a hole in the ground. Once inside, the rabbit would invariably bump into a trigger precariously protruding through the upper wall of the box, thereby releasing a wooden door behind the animal which trapped him inside the hollow tunnel. The rabbit would then be taken from the wooden box and killed.

While younger brother Manson usually credits Bill with having been the most successful box rabbit trapper in Cove, Manson decided at an early age to try the method himself. He borrowed a couple of box traps from Bill and headed for the woods where he made a couple of what he considered very likely sets. Upon checking the traps the following morning, he was elated to find that one of them contained a large swamp rabbit. Eager to get the animal out of the box, he neglected to locate a club with which to strike the rabbit over the head. Instead, he quickly lifted the wooden door, thrust his hand inside and caught the rabbit by the scruff of the neck, much as one would pick up a kitten, and dragged the enraged animal outside.

Once out of the box where the rodent had greater freedom of movement, the fight commenced immediately. The rabbit furiously clawed Manson's forearm with rapid, slashing movements of its back feet. Unwilling to release his hold on the rabbit, but realizing he was going to have to do something quickly, the boy took off in a run toward home, the rabbit flailing the air and slashing the boy's arm every step of the way. Before reaching the house, Manson noticed blood dripping from his arm and severe pain enveloped the slashed area. The rabbit continued his relentless battle for freedom, now stretching his hind legs almost to the boy's elbow and carving slices out of the arm with each recoil. Finally, discretion became the better part of valor and Manson released his hold on the animal. The rabbit's legs already well in motion when it struck the ground, it took little time to scamper away, leaving young Manson with an empty hand and a bloody arm.

Manson was not quite ten years of age when the devastating hurricane of 1915 struck the upper Texas coast. Old-timers of the area said the wind blew more fiercely and the tides rose higher than had been the case in 1900, when a violent hurricane practically destroyed Galveston and several surrounding communities. The 1915 blow was more often compared to that of 1875, which wreaked a great deal of destruction in the Galveston and Trinity bays region.

The 1915 hurricane pushed tides in excess of fifteen feet above normal level, inundating the entire expanse of the marshlands. Approximately one half of the trees in portions of the Cove woods were toppled by the furious winds, and salt spray from the Gulf waters was driven so far inland as to cause metal objects on the highland to rust away in the fields and yards of farmers. Manson's mother, Florence Clark, had just received a new wood-burning cook stove, but had not as yet had it installed. Setting on the front porch of the Clark home, the stove was completely rusted by the salty spray driven by the hurricane's winds.

As the wind gradually subsided the following day, Manson followed the elder William down to the home of their neighbor, Zachary T. "Zack" Maley, who resided on the northern shore of Cotton Lake. While the grown folks were inside drinking coffee and exchanging tales of the previous night's big blow, Manson strolled down toward the mouth of Spring Branch Gully, just east of Zack's house, and saw something that made his heart jump. Laying in the driftwood and debris left by the storm tides along the hillside was an object which had the appearance of a baby's head. Word had already been circulated about a number of people killed and missing in the storm and Manson just knew he had found one. Racing back to the house, he burst inside and related in excited tones the sighting of the baby's head in the drift. William, Zack and Owen Maley, Zack's oldest son, dashed out of the house toward the scene of the supposedly morbid discovery. Manson pointed to the round object across the pile of logs, sea cane and timbers, and the men cautiously made their way across the tangled mess, watching carefully for displaced, angry cottonmouth moccasins. Upon reaching the point where Manson had indicated, the three men reared back in hilarious laughter. Close investigation had revealed the object to be only a round bulb-shaped root of a prickly pear plant, apparently uprooted from one of the marsh islands and blown ashore. Young Manson was somewhat embarrassed by the turn of his discovery, but the effects of the hurricane would remain with him for many years to come.

Despite the destruction wrought by the 1915 hurricane, the storm did have its positive side. The same winds and tides which brought so much devastation to the coastal region also brought a new form of wildlife to the Cove area marshlands. Several muskrats were washed into the marshes, believed to have been snatched from the swamps of Louisiana by the swirling torrents of wind and water and hurled ashore in Texas. However, the nature of the counter-clockwise cyclonic winds of a hurricane suggest this could not have been the case. It is more likely they came from an area more south or west of the hurricane's path. But regardless of their origin, they were now in the Cove marshes. As the storm moved inland, the wind gradually abated and the tides receded back toward the Gulf of Mexico, the furry little grayish-black rodents began rapid adaptation to their new home. As their numbers increased in the marshes during the following two to three years, they shared with Cove its part in an era which has come to be known in the history of the American fur industry as "The Golden Age of Fur Trapping." The muskrat himself would come to bear the distinction as "the trapper's meal ticket." Manson Clark, as well as several other young men of the Cove area, would learn to take advantage of this period in our history and convert it into a way of life for themselves and their families.

William Clark usually kept a couple boats moored on the north shore of Cotton Lake near the homes of Zack and Joseph Maley, both sons of early Cove settler, William Maley. On various occasions, sport hunters would make their way from Houston and other distant points along the muddy roads leading to Cove and pay the elder Clark for the rent of a rowing skiff with which to enter the marshes for the purpose of duck hunting during the fall and winter months. One of Clark's neighbors, George B. Wilburn, had already begun to earn a few dollars by acting as a guide for some of these "city slickers" who were willing to pay for such services.

Manson's older brother, Bill, was sent by the elder William into the marshes with some of these hunters to assist them in crossing the lake to the marshes beyond. On one such excursion, Bill and a hunter were returning from across Cotton Lake and nearing the north shore where the boat was again to be securely moored. As was common during the winter months in the inland bay areas, the tide was running at quite a low level on this particular day and the boat began to drag upon the lake bottom as they neared the shore. Bill stepped overboard into the muddy shore water and took a firm grip on the mooring rope attached to the bow of the boat in order to pull the skiff to shore so the sportsman could exit the boat without bogging through too much excessive mud. As he prepared to tug at the skiff, Bill noticed the novice hunter standing upright in the boat and stepping onto the rear seat near the stern, his hands upon his hips and his eyes scanning the shoreline. "How stupid can anybody be?", Bill thought. "When I pull this boat, that fella is likely to lose his balance and fall overboard." The longer Bill envisioned that thought, the more it intrigued him. Unable to withstand the temptation, Bill planted his feet solidly in the cold mud and gave a tremendous jerk on the rope. As the skiff suddenly broke loose from the lake bottom and lurched forward, the man perched upon the rear seat of the boat appeared to perform a perfect backward swan dive. His feet were lifted into the air at about the same level as his head, his body assuming a prone position in mid-air. Then, down he came, flat on his back.

As he struck the surface of the water, it suddenly opened on either side of him, reminding Bill of the manner in which God had rolled back the waters of the Red Sea to allow Moses and the children of Israel to escape their pursuers so many centuries ago. Then, just as quickly, the water closed back across the man as he sank below the muddy surface. Bill had a difficult time in concealing his delight at the spectacle, but managed to hold his countenance so that the city hunter believed it had all been a mistake.

William Clark had viewed the entire episode from the hillside as he and Joe Maley stood watching over the lake. Never one to allow one of his sons to get away with such a stunt, William broke a limb from a tree and waited for Bill and the hunter to climb the hillside, where he intended to give his eldest son a severe thrashing. As the couple approached, William started toward Bill with the limb, informing him he had seen everything that had happened at the lakeshore and he was about to pay dearly for his action. At that point, the sportsman intervened. The man pleaded with the older man not to whip Bill, that he (the hunter) had gotten exactly what he deserved. "Anyone stupid enough to stand on a boat seat when the boat is about to move deserves to get all wet," the hunter said. With the matter thus resolved, they all began to laugh and talk of the comical manner in which the hunter had gone into the mud and water of the lake.

The winter of 1918-19 was a colder-than-normal period for southeast Texas. An especially frigid "blue norther" swept through the region in January, sending temperatures below the freezing point for several days and coated Cotton Lake with a thin sheet of ice from shore to shore. Standing on the lakeshore one day during the phenomenal freeze, Manson detected small round holes in the ice scattered at various intervals across the lake. Curious as to what might be causing these odd breaks in the otherwise solid sheet of ice, he took a wooden skiff from its mooring, turned its bow toward the center of the lake and, holding onto the stern of the small vessel, began to wade out into the chilly mud and water. Using the boat to break the ice before him, he arrived at the closest hole in the ice and found a buffalo fish floating at the surface, completely numbed from the cold water. Manson found that he could pick the fish up from the water and toss it into the boat without the creature even so much as flouncing about in his hand. "Gracious!", he thought. "If there is a fish in every one of those holes in the ice, I'd better get busy." And on to the next hole he went, pushing the skiff before him. He also found some catfish in some of the holes, in the same physical condition as the buffalo. Traveling from one break in the ice to the next, leaving a trail of broken ice behind him, he soon had all the buffalo and catfish the little skiff would haul, so he headed back toward the north shore of the lake. Cleaning his "catch" and shipping the fish to market, it really made the thirteen-year-old boy feel like a man that he was able to add some money to the family coffers. Never again would Manson have an opportunity to acquire so many fish in this manner, but it was an experience he would recall countless times in future years as he sought both buffalo and catfish with nets, seines and trot lines.

The lifestyle of Manson and his brothers and sisters during the early, formative years of their lives was not unlike that of most other children and families of rural Cove during the early 1900's. The majority of the children of that period attended school long enough to learn the basic skills of reading, writing and arithmetic which was considered ample education to see them through the trials of life. Manson's favorite subject in school was always history. The study of the early pioneers fascinated him, especially as it related to the settlement of Texas. Perhaps his fascination with the life of the pioneer, combined with the lifestyle of sparsely-settled Cove, provided some motivation in his choice of an occupation as he approached manhood.

In the fall of 1919, Clyde Maley and Manson, both fourteen- year-old boys and lifelong neighbors in Cove, made a duck hunting trip in the marshes between Cross Bayou and the lower reaches of Old River Lake. Rowing their skiff down the then narrow bends of the bayou, they turned eastward into Cane Pond Slough, sometimes known locally as "Little Coley," and paddled to a point near Cane Pond where they beached the boat. Clyde threw out a few decoys on the pond and situated himself in a blind on the shore while Manson struck out to "walk up" some ducks across the marsh toward Old River Lake. Manson did not flush any ducks out of the potholes in his trek across the marsh, but an occasional shot back in the direction of Cane Pond told him that Clyde was having a bit of luck.

Manson bogged all the way to the southern shore of Old River Lake, getting his pants wet to a point above the knees when crossing a slough. Upon reaching the lakeshore, he stopped to rest a few minutes. Then, he saw a skiff coming across the lake toward him. The boat moved along at a pace which would be natural for a good oarsman, but he saw no sign of oars protruding from either side of the boat. As the vessel neared the shore, he heard the unmistakable sound of a gasoline engine. As it reached the shore, he saw there were three uniformed men aboard, the boat propelled by a one-cylinder outboard motor on the stern of the vessel. "What luxury!" the teenager thought, "coming across the lake like that without even having to use the oars."

The bow of the skiff beached on the muddy lakeshore and the operator shut off the engine. The three men identified themselves as game wardens, the first such officers Manson had ever seen. They checked him for ducks and Manson accommodated their every request, but he could not seem to keep his eyes off the engine on the stern of their boat. Satisfied that he was well within the law on all counts, they were curious to know how he had reached this location on the lakeshore on foot, and he motioned with a sweep of his arm back across the marshes through which he had traveled.

The conversation then turned to their presence on Old River Lake. Where had they come from? The men replied they had come from Galveston, across Galveston and Trinity bays, into the Trinity River, and finally into the lower reaches of Old River which led them to the lake and this spot where the young hunter stood. They indicated they would like to find Cross Bayou and follow it back to Trinity Bay from which point they could begin their trip back to Galveston. Manson immediately saw in this an opportunity to avoid the boggy walk back across the marsh and, more importantly, to ride in a boat propelled by mechanical power. He offered to show them the route to Cross Bayou if they would allow him to ride with them as far as Cane Pond Slough where his boat was tied. The men accepted the offer and the foursome entered the mouth of Hugo Bayou, the stream which ultimately led them to Cross Bayou, just southeast of Cotton Lake.

Manson was grateful for the ride, but even more grateful for the opportunity to have witnessed firsthand the actual operation of an outboard motor. He declared then and there that he would someday have one of those contraptions himself, little realizing that the day would come when outboard motors would become the primary source of transportation in the waters and marshes of Cove and elsewhere. But for now, in 1919, he really had a story to tell Clyde after he made his way back to the duck blind.

In later years, Manson would readily confess that he would probably have gotten more education, or at least have gotten more out of the education he did receive, had his mind not always been outside the classroom. After all, his father, William, was a member of the Cove school board so he could not claim his parents were apathetic about schooling. He just could not keep from thinking about a new trapset he had made along a gully bank that morning. During the fall months, the sound outside the school windows of the early geese arriving from their summer retreat in Canada always caused him to pause over his studies and listen to the plaintive sound of the big waterfowl as they winged their way over the highland and into the Cove marshes. That sound heralded new life into the blood of the young men of Cove as the cool weather of fall gradually replaced the incessant heat of the waning summer. While numerous school days were missed by the young truants during the late spring and early fall months of the year for the purpose of helping in the planting and picking of the family cotton fields, Manson's desk was also frequently empty at times during the winter months as he was lured outdoors by the call of the woods and marshes.

Manson completed his sixth year of education at age fourteen. Like many young Cove men his age, he considered that to be sufficient education and determined that he was now of an age to be responsible enough to add a few dollars to the family till. Through his early years he had received his training along the gullies in the woods and the shores of Cotton Lake. To his way of thinking, it was now time to put that training to work. It was, therefore, at the age of fourteen that Manson Clark ventured into the life of an outdoorsman which would become the mainstay of his family for decades to come.

▪ CHAPTER II ▪

TRIALS OF THE WILDLIFE PROFESSION

Manson had watched with interest through his boyhood years as men came to the Clark home from areas around Houston, paid William for the rent of a boat, and went into the marshes to hunt ducks and geese. He was often amused by their antics in attempting to handle a skiff with a pair of oars on the open waters of Cotton Lake and the pathetic wailings and groanings of their duck calling techniques as they attempted to lure the waterfowl within shooting range. In 1919, he began offering his services to the hunters for fifty cents per day. In earning the money, Manson would row the men across the lake in a skiff, position them in a blind or patch of sea cane, call the ducks in over the decoys for them, and row them back to the highland after the completion of the hunt. It was tiring work, but since he usually managed to get in a bit of shooting of his own, it all seemed worthwhile. And besides, he always carried one of his mother's delicious baked sweet potatoes in the pocket of his coat when on such excursions, the morsel giving him additional energy when he needed it most.

One of his first such expeditions with the sport hunters came about rather accidentally. Ed Hill, one of Manson's closest friends and hunting partners in Cove, had spent the night with him and the two boys intended to go duck hunting the following morning. Out of bed before daylight, they found that three men from Houston had just arrived at the Clark home with their hearts set on making a hunt that day. Manson's father, William, and older brother, Bill, were temporarily away from home on some business of the elder Clark, so Manson told the men he and Ed would take them to the marshes. Hurriedly preparing for the day's activity, Manson did not neglect to secure his usual baked sweet potato and stick it into his coat pocket as the party left the house.

It was quite a warm morning for duck hunting as the five crowded into the rowing skiff on the north shore of Cotton Lake before the break of day. Besides Manson and Ed, the party consisted of Jim Hanks, Fred Miller, and Orville Briggs. The sky was overcast and a light to moderate southeasterly wind allowed for an average tide in the lake. Not too bad a day for hunting, the men mused as they crossed the lake to the rhythmic sound of Manson's oars cutting the surface of the water. Reaching the south bank of the lake, the boat was pulled partially out of the water and onto the shore to

22

avoid its drifting away during their hunt in the marsh. The three visitors gathered up their shotguns, shells and other accoutrements while Manson shouldered a sackful of decoys for the walk to Wet Marsh Pond, about a quarter of a mile distant across the boggy terrain. The hunters walked to various points in the area to await the early morning flight of waterfowl. Hanks went into a blind on the edge of the pond while Miller and Briggs squatted in the sea cane to await daybreak. Ed, knowing the area almost as well as Manson, headed farther back into the marshes to a pothole where he thought he might have some good shooting.

At daybreak, a few ducks began working the area as the southerly winds increased in velocity. "If the wind whips up brisk enough this morning," Manson told one of the hunters, "it might break up some of those rafts of ducks on the bay and cause them to look for shelter in the marsh," thereby providing the hunters a better opportunity for some spirited shooting. As the sun prepared to make its debut for the day, its rays lighting the eastern horizon, Manson noticed a dark, heavy cloud emerging over the hillside on the north side of Cotton Lake. It stretched as far as the eye could see, from east to west, and appeared to be creeping southward toward the marshes. Manson walked back to the boat at the lakeshore to retrieve his shotgun, but paused there to watch the rapid approach of the leading edge of the cloud. Suddenly, a frigid north wind struck the shore and the waters on the lake went wild, the waves on the surface having changed direction and now beating the south bank of the lake. "What a norther!" Manson thought as the sudden gusts of wind almost blew him off balance. The sea cane swayed and bent southward under the force of the gale.

After a couple hours during which the wind showed no sign of diminishing, but rather seemed to increase in intensity, Manson decided he and his hunters had better prepare to leave and try to reach the north side of the lake and home before the north wind blew the tidewater out to such a low ebb that they would have difficulty in navigating the shallow lake. About that time, Miller and Ed came trudging out of the marsh, ready to give it up for the day. But where were Briggs and Hanks? A fine mist had already begun falling and was now taking on more the appearance of sleet. Miller said he thought Briggs had caught a ride in a rowboat with some other men leaving the marshes through a bayou some time ago, which indicated to Manson that Briggs might have left the area with some of George Wilburn's hunters who had also been out that morning. That realization left only Hanks unaccounted for. Having been in the blind on Wet Marsh Pond, he was nearest the lakeshore and should have been back at the boat by now. Manson would walk back to the blind and look for the man.

Approaching the blind, the mud about his bare feet now becoming colder by the minute, Manson found Hanks lying down on some cane in the bottom of the blind, a pile of dead ducks beside him. "Get up," he told the man, "before you freeze to death!" Hanks was sound asleep, his knees drawn up before him in an obvious effort to keep warm. Manson shook the man, even resorting to kicking him with his bare feet, to finally rouse him from his cold slumber. Getting Hanks to his feet, Manson picked up the hunter's gun and ducks and told the freezing man to follow him back to the boat. With the string of ducks over one shoulder, Manson found he had to support part of Hanks' weight with the other as the hunter leaned on the boy for balance while they bogged back toward the boat. Hanks kept muttering words which became inaudible in the howling wind, but Manson figured the words had no meaning anyhow as Hanks seemed almost out of his mind from the cold.

Reaching the skiff on the lakeshore, they found Miller and Ed walking in circles in an effort to keep warm. The wind was now blowing at such a rate that the biting cold seemed to cut through their bodies. Ed's face, hands and feet were beginning to take on a different shade from the effects of the cold wind. In an effort to escape the wind briefly, the men pulled the boat out on the bank and turned it up on its side, propping it with oars, and squatted down behind its southward side for temporary relief from the wind. Discussing their plight, they agreed they could not remain there much longer as the tide was now obviously falling at a rapid pace.

Turning the boat back onto its bottom, they shoved it into the waters of the lake, the waves splashing over the side as they slowly pushed the skiff away from the bank in the breakers. Climbing into the boat, Manson took his position on the middle seat and tugged at the oars. With Miller and Ed on the rear seat and the frigid Hanks in the bow, it was a slow, tedious pace which began to carry them back across Cotton Lake. Manson was beginning to feel a bit better now, the exertion of working the oars bringing new warmth to his body. Miller reached forward from the rear seat and, grasping the oars with Manson, added more power to their slow progress. Manson's innate love of wildlife remained as he could not keep his eyes off the swarms of ducks which now appeared flying low over the angry waters, the fowl seeking a place where they might escape the wind. Ed sat very still and Manson worried about his good friend's physical condition. Hanks, perched upon the seat in the bow of the skiff, was now almost completely irrational, staring at the floor of the boat and continuously muttering words and sounds to himself, none of which meant anything to the others in the boat.

By mid-afternoon, the foursome had progressed slightly more than halfway across the lake, the violent wind seeming to drive them backward after each tug at the oars. Suddenly, another skiff appeared on the lake, coming toward them from the north shore. It approached rapidly, travelling with the wind, and Manson soon recognized the two men as his father, William, and Ed's father, Eli Hill. Concerned about the safety of their sons, William and Eli had borrowed a skiff from Joe Maley to row out on the windswept lake and lend a helping hand to the fatigued party. The boats coming alongside each other and tossed wildly about by the waves, Ed numbly crawled into the skiff with the two elder men and both vessels were again turned northward into the wind for the final distance to the shore.

Late in the afternoon, the boats and their weary passengers finally beached on the north shore of Cotton Lake. Mooring the skiffs securely to old, weather-beaten posts, the men and boys began the walk across the narrow stretch of marsh to the hillside and home. Manson then remembered that he had not even taken time during the busy day to eat his baked potato. Pulling it from his coat pocket, he had just begun to remove the peeling when Jim Hanks, now almost insane from the cold, spotted the morsel. Instantly, he grasped the potato from Manson's hand and gobbled it down, peeling and all. He then continued his trek toward the hillside, staring blindly ahead as if he had done nothing out of the ordinary. Manson did not say a word to Hanks about the matter. He could not help but feel compassion for this man whose normal senses had been so cruelly stifled by the numbing cold.

Upon reaching the Clark home, William invited them all inside for the first really comfortable minutes they had experienced since the early morning hours of the day. There was Briggs, already warmed inside the house after having come in earlier with George Wilburn's hunters, and now having a hot cup of coffee with Florence. An appearance of instant relief showered the party as they entered the warmth of the house from the bitter cold outside. Florence scurried into the kitchen to pour more cups of hot coffee. Hanks suddenly caught sight of the fireplace on the far side of the living room, the flames leaping upward into the chimney from the crackling logs. Instantly, he made a lunge toward the brick enclosure and was about to bodily enter the fire when William and Eli caught hold of his clothing and wrestled him away from the fireplace, Hanks all the while whimpering like a scolded puppy. Due to this act of near insanity on Hanks' part, William suggested they all go into another room of the house where they, and especially Hanks, could warm up slowly and there would be no open fire to lure Hanks.

Finally warmed by the coffee and a dry change of clothes, the group sat around the fireplace and discussed the morning's ordeal. Even Hanks was again coming to his senses and was embarrassed when told of some of his escapades of the day. Later, as the three hunters prepared to leave Cove for their return trip to Houston, the men told William that had his son not known the right things to do when the blizzard struck them in the marsh that morning, they might have all frozen to death on the south shore of Cotton Lake. After a round of hand-shaking among the men, they began filing out of the house to their car outside. Hanks paused in the doorway, turned back to William and said, "Mr. Clark, the next time I go duck hunting, it will be on a hot day in the middle of July! "

■　■　■　■　■　■　■

During the few years since a few muskrats had been washed into the Cove marshes by the 1915 hurricane, the furry little creatures had experienced excellent water and weather conditions to thrive and reproduce in number. As the fall and winter months approached, a few of Cove's young men became aware of a market demand for the fur of the muskrat, which gave them yet another incentive to spend more time in the marshlands. In those early, infant days of taking muskrats in the Cove marshes, shotguns were used to shoot them off the tops of their beds, or nests, which were now appearing all over the marshes. This method did not long endure, however, as it soon became readily evident that a much better grade of furs without the pellet holes from the gun blasts would bring more money on the market. Recognition of this fact soon replaced the shotgun with the steel trap in the taking of the varmints.

Of all the marshland fur bearers, the muskrat has some of the strangest characteristics. Weather conditions sometime appear to control the animal's every thought and motion. Practically dormant during the hot summer season, the 'rats begin to stir about as the first northers of the fall push their way southward across the Texas coast. The muskrat's lair, usually referred to in southeast Texas as a "bed", is allowed to fall into a state of disarray during the warm season. As long as the weather is hot, the muskrat will hardly venture outside the bed to gnaw down a few stalks of sea cane or twill grass to patch his home. It is this state of relative hibernation during the summer months which often spells doom for entire colonies of muskrats in the marshes during long summer droughts. As the watery tunnels leading into the base of the bed dry up, taking with it the animal's natural water supply for the summer, he will rarely travel farther than thirty or forty feet from the bed in search of water and, consequently, will die of thirst. Doubtless, it is for this reason that the instinct of the muskrat causes him to prefer the lowest, wettest sections of the marshlands as sites for the construction of the beds.

26

When the northers begin arriving in the fall, and increasing in regularity and severity during the winter, the 'rat appears to become almost obsessed with activity. He first begins to set his house back in order, carrying bits of grass and mud in his teeth for the refurbishing process. A pair of the little grayish-black rodents will often construct a bed of some three feet in height and five feet in diameter during a single overnight period. Once the bed is back in proper condition, the muskrat again becomes quite particular about the weather into which he ventures. Cove trappers have noted through the years that the muskrat prefers the temperature to range between 35 and 45 degrees as it is during such nights that the best catches of the 'rats are made. The experienced trapper soon learns not to set his traps too near the beds for fear of catching the small, younger members of the muskrat family which normally travel only a few feet from the bed. Although the muskrat matures rapidly and is very prolific in preferable conditions, the trapper realizes that the young 'rats are the "seed" for the following year's crop.

When Manson took to the marshes during the winter of 1918-19 with a dozen steel traps, he had visions of successful catches of muskrats on a daily basis. It did not take long, however, for that thought to become shattered. He had gone into the marshes around Horse Island, south of Cotton Lake, and made sets in every trail he found. The following morning was quite a disappointment as he found that only one of his traps had secured a 'rat. This process was repeated for several consecutive nights and he was about ready to give up this new enterprise. Then, one morning while running his trap line, and looking for other areas in which to make some sets, he chanced to run upon Dempsey Reeves. Dempsey was an older man, a resident of the Old River community, and already had a winter or two of experience in trapping the elusive little 'rats. He gave Manson some pointers, such as searching for the freshest 'rat trails, or "runs," that were most often used by the animals. Manson took Dempsey at his word and began employing some of the techniques the older man had shown him. His daily catch increased noticeably and Manson began to learn what the feeling was, and is, to get trapping "in the blood."

One morning during his early trapping days, Manson had caught a number of muskrats and returned from the marsh to his boat, securely tied to a stake on the south shore of Cotton Lake. Noting that the wind was from a southeasterly direction, he determined that he could allow his boat to drift with the breeze which would carry him back to near the point where he kept the skiff moored on the north side of the lake. While drifting across the body of water, he would avail himself of the opportunity to skin his morning catch.

Sitting on the middle seat of the boat, Manson busied himself with removing the skins from the muskrats as the wind carried him nearer and nearer to home. He was learning the points of making every movement with his knife count to advantage in the skinning process, a method which years later would enable him to remove the skins from two muskrats per minute. As he worked at the task, he completed the skinning of each animal by pulling the hide off the nose of the 'rat with one hand and tossing the carcass overboard with the other, where it would be devoured by hungry marine predators. Each skin was then placed in the bottom of the boat. This process was repeated until the last 'rat was skinned, at which time the trapper would lean over the side of the skiff and wash the furs in the lake waters. Usually, by the time he had completed the entire job, his boat would be nearing the north shoreline, whereupon he would secure an oar to guide the skiff to its point of landing. During one such morning of the skinning process, Manson pulled the hide off a rat and, without noticing which hand held the skinning knife, threw the carcass into the lake, only to notice to his chagrin that his knife plummeted into the lake along with the muskrat carcass. The knife apparently remains in the muddy bottom of Cotton Lake to this day as he was unable to retrieve the instrument from the mud and water.

Back at home with his morning's catch of furs, Manson used heavy gauge wire, such as was used to construct family clotheslines, on which to place the furs for the drying procedure. The wire was cut into pieces of some 36 to 40 inches in length, each piece being bent into the shape of a horseshoe. Once the fur was dried, the pelts were inverted, with the fur turned inside, and pulled over the stretchers. The excess meat was cut from the raw hide and the pelt was set outside to cure. Muskrat skins would dry in a day's time if clear, dry weather prevailed. Manson also whittled out a few thin boards in the desired shape and size for use as stretchers, but always found that the wire was best suited for the purpose.

Upon acquiring a total of one hundred dried pelts, the young trapper wrapped them all up one day and carried them to the Cove post office, located at Joseph's Store on the west bank of Old River Lake. From here, he shipped his catch to Funsten Fur Company in St. Louis, Missouri. William had complained quite a bit during the past few weeks about his son spending so much time in the marshes and working with the furs, believing the boy was only wasting his time, because no one wanted to buy the skins of a bunch of filthy rodents. After a few weeks, Manson had begun to think his elder might be correct as he waited day after day for a reply from Funsten. Finally one day, an envelope arrived at the post office from the fur company, addressed to "Manson Clark, Cove, Texas."

The boy hurriedly tore open the envelope and inside found a check in the amount of fifty dollars. That amounted to fifty cents "a round" for his furs! This amount was a considerable lump of money in 1919. The boy rushed over the distance back home and excitedly showed William the check. The elder man's view on his son's fur trapping suddenly shifted to one of a more positive nature and he urged Manson to set more traps in the marsh. It was now, however, too late for that. Spring had arrived with its warm weather and trapping was over for the year.

Manson eagerly looked forward to the following fall and winter as he went through the summer drudgery of helping plant, chop and pick the year's cotton crop. 1919 had begun as a very wet year in which many local farmers had not even been able to get their seeds in the ground in time to begin raising the annual crop. During the summer, however, weather conditions turned off extremely dry and hot. Week after week, farmers watched the heavens for any sign of rain-producing clouds, but none appeared until later that fall, and by then it was too late for many of the crops. Wide cracks crisscrossed the baked earth and the "black gumbo" soil became as hard as concrete. Vegetation died and with it went a substantial portion of the year's crops.

■　■　■　■　■　■　■

When Manson returned to the marshes with his traps that fall, he found that the dry conditions had taken a toll on the lowlands as well. Even the usually wet, muddy marshlands had dried up during the summer drought. The muskrats which had appeared so plentiful the previous winter simply were not there this year. Many had died of starvation, unwilling to leave their beds in the hot weather to travel far enough to reach water, although the bayous and deeper sloughs had felt the invasion of salt water from the bay during the dry spell and, therefore, was unfit for drinking. Others, finding the marsh floor too hard to dig for roots near their beds, had resorted to eating some of the remaining green sprouts of grass above the surface of the ground. Being unaccustomed to such a diet, the 'rats soon developed diarrhea which killed them in countless numbers.

One of Manson's older sisters, Elsie, had married in the spring of 1915 to Tillman Fitzgerald, a member of the pioneer Fitzgerald family of Barbers Hill. During his younger years, Tillman was quite an avid outdoorsman and especially enjoyed various forms of hunting. Marrying into the Clark family of Cove gave him an opportunity to exercise such activities all the more. Although he and Elsie resided at

Barbers Hill, they spent as much time in Cove as possible, where Tillman found his brothers-in-law ready to take him on trips into the marsh with them for just about any outdoor excursion.

One morning in the late fall of 1919, Manson and Tillman crawled from beneath their bed covers in the wee hours of the post-midnight morning and headed down Cross Bayou in a rowboat, or "pulling skiff," to do some duck hunting that day. About five miles down the winding stream, not far from its mouth at Trinity Bay, they pulled the boat into the bank on the east side and began their walk across the marsh, directly toward the point where the sun would be rising in less than an hour. Their destination was a big pond Manson knew about where they anticipated some good duck shooting during the morning. The water over the marsh where they walked was about ankle deep and the marsh grass grew to the height of their knees. When they left the boat, Manson had taken the lead since he knew the whereabouts of the pond and could find it in the darkness. Tillman followed along behind, the two young men saying not a word and walking as quietly as possible in an effort not to break the quietness of an early morning on the marsh.

As they walked along slowly, Manson recalled his coon trapping brother, Bill, having told him there had been quite a number of coons in this area recently, and the early predawn darkness was always a good time to flush one of the old masked bandits out of the grass. Without mentioning this thought to Tillman, Manson began watching closely in the grass ahead for a possible sighting of a coon. Suddenly, he noticed some movement in the grass some twenty-five feet directly ahead. It was still dark, but he could faintly detect the breaking of the shallow water at the point of the moving grass. They had jumped a coon, Manson thought, and it was trotting along right in front of them. Quietly slipping a load of No. 5 shot into his shotgun, Manson put the weapon to his shoulder, pulled back the hammer, and took aim at the splashing water at his front. As he was about to squeeze the trigger, Tillman cleared his throat – at exactly the same spot where Manson had taken aim. It was not a coon after all, but rather was Tillman, who had somehow passed Manson undetected along their route and had taken the lead. Manson felt weak from head to toe, and later said, "My heart went into my throat. If he (Tillman) hadn't cleared his throat when he did, I would have shot his feet off. I realized it all in one instant. Oh, what a lesson that was I have never forgotten."

Manson himself came close to being on the receiving end of a shotgun blast one day when he and Bill had been hunting in the fields behind the Joe Maley property.

Finishing their hunt, they were walking home through a portion of the Maley property known locally as "The Lane," a narrow strip of land bounded on the south by the land of the Winfree family. Bill was in the lead and Manson walked along behind his older brother. Bill had acquired a habit of walking along with his empty gun over his shoulder, muzzle to the rear, cocking the weapon and pulling the trigger at intervals. This day, as the two brothers headed for home, Bill went through the same ritual, the only difference being that he had neglected to unload his gun when they completed the hunt. The result was a blast above Manson's shoulder and to the left side of his head. Not a pellet of the shot touched him, but the deafening ringing in his ears kept him from being able to hear Bill's feverish inquiries as to whether or not he had been hit with any of the shot. Bill likewise learned an important lesson that day.

On yet another occasion, Manson had been on another hunting jaunt and had returned from the marshes, docking his boat at the wharf behind Joseph's Store on the west bank of Old River Lake. Stepping from the boat, he tied the mooring rope to the wharf and turned back to the boat to retrieve his shotgun. Grasping the weapon by the end of the barrel, he pulled it toward him, the muzzle pointed directly at his face. Uncomfortable with looking down the barrel of what he thought was an empty gun, he moved the muzzle slightly to the right and gave it a jerk as it seemed to catch on something in the boat. The hammer had lodged on the boat seat, causing the minor resistance, and as he suddenly tugged at the barrel, the hammer slipped from the edge of the seat, slammed shut against the firing mechanism, and the shot roared past his head with sudden thundering reverberation. He escaped this near shot of death with only some powder burns on the side of the head.

■　■　■　■　■　■　■

The summer of 1920 brought yet another new facet of marsh life for Manson. He had learned of a market for alligator hides and wanted to try his hand in this field. Since Sears-Roebuck and Company was the primary source for just about everything not raised on the farm or purchased in local country stores, Manson wrote to the firm for a piece of equipment necessary in the sometimes dangerous practice of alligator hunting. He sent off his order for a Bulls-Eye II brand headlight, then anxiously awaited its delivery at the post office at Joseph's Store. After what seemed an eternity, the package finally arrived in the mail one day during the middle of the summer, and Manson headed home with the merchandise. The light was fueled by signal oil and came equipped with an adjustable headband for fitting around the hunter's cap.

Late in the afternoon, he gathered the headlight, a jar of drinking water, and his 12-gauge shotgun, and excitedly made his way to his boat on Cotton Lake. Rowing southward across the lake to Alligator (or Gougee) Bayou, he arrived at the mouth of the stream about sunset. Sitting in the boat amid the stillness of the marsh evening, he strapped the light to his head. As the darkness deepened, he switched on the light and allowed his eyes to become accustomed to the narrow beam which cut through the black night before him. Slipping a shell into the shotgun, Manson positioned himself on the rear seat of the boat so that he could row the skiff while scanning the bayou ahead of the boat with the light beam.

Pushing the oars as silently as possible, Manson had hardly become accustomed to his position when suddenly a bright red spot appeared in the beam of light near the bayou bank ahead. The alligator's eye glowed like a red-hot chunk of burning coal against the background of the dark, earthen bank. Excited with the prospect of a reward for his night's effort, he raised the gun, lined up the barrel with the beam of light, and fired. The blast suddenly broke the stillness of the night and frogs and night birds croaked and chattered with excitement for a few seconds. Then, all was again silent on the ancient waterway. Quietly paddling the skiff to the spot where the 'gator had been, Manson probed the mud and water with an oar to locate the reptile, but it was nowhere to be found. Surely, he could not have missed such a motionless target–not with a shotgun. Disappointed by the results of this initial opportunity, he nevertheless moved farther down the bayou in search of more alligators. Fourteen additional times the same process was repeated; the 'gator was spotted, the shot rang out, but he had nothing to show for his attempts, except a maze of mosquito bites on his bare arms and feet.

Manson had begun the evening hunt with a total of twenty shotgun shells, but now had only five left. He considered saving those remaining shells for duck hunting the next fall and simply giving up this alligator business as a valiant, but vain, experiment. As he turned the skiff around in the bayou to begin rowing back toward the lake, the red glow of another 'gator eye suddenly caught his attention in the beam of light. The reptile was hardly twenty feet away from the boat and Manson was surprised to have rowed so near the animal without scaring him away. Again, he slowly raised the gun and fired. A sudden splashing of mud and water sent ripples against the side of the skiff. Then, the surface of the bayou again lay smooth. Feeling the bayou bottom with the boat oar, he felt the wooden paddle strike the hard, scaly hide of the 'gator. Lifting the reptile from the bayou and into the skiff, Manson then realized that the beam from the headlight would allow him to approach to within close range of the animals, insuring a clean kill with each shot.

Rowing back up the bayou, Manson spotted four more alligators with the light and silently pushed the skiff up to within close range of each, and made killing shots with each of his remaining shells. That was the secret, he thought as he neared the mouth of the bayou at the lake. They have to be shot at close range or the pellets of the shot simply will not penetrate the tough hides and bony heads of the 'gators. Sighting several more alligators before reaching the mouth of the bayou and emerging onto the waters of Cotton Lake, he wished he had had this knowledge when he had entered the bayou with his twenty shells earlier in the evening. But, that was all a part of learning, he convinced himself as he rowed the skiff laden with the five reptiles back across the lake in the darkness. There would be other alligators.

CHAPTER III

THE 1920's

The decade of the 1920's in America brought post-World War I prosperity to much of the nation, even if it later proved to be a false sense of security. The country wrestled with Prohibition, looser morals, the Ku Klux Klan, and women voters. While times changed drastically over most of the nation, not much real difference in lifestyle affected the everyday life in conservative and rural Cove, Texas.

The decade had begun in southeast Texas with a drought which caused numerous farmers to be forced to forego their planting for the year. When the heavens finally did open later in the year, the rains were plentiful, so much so that the water-logged ground became the next problem. As the rains continued, with the earth unable to soak up anymore of the water in 1920, the Trinity River inevitably began a major rise. The muddy waters rushed southward down the ancient stream to the coastal marshlands, covering the marshes and creating a virtual bay from Cove to the Gulf of Mexico. Cove residents lay in their beds at night, listening to the rush of water over the slightly higher shore of Trinity Bay several miles to the south. Such were the days when the river remained unobstructed by man-made dams farther upstream.

In the Cove marshes, the several weeks of rushing water proved disastrous to the muskrat population. The 'rat beds were washed away and most of the little rodents were drowned. When the rains slacked off during the late fall and the river gradually began to recede back within its banks, it became obvious to those concerned about the matter that there would be no muskrat trapping for several years to come. The young men of Cove who had adopted the work of trapping in the lowlands as a means of livelihood realized they would have to turn to other forms of work to pay the bills this year.

Rabbit hunting had been somewhat of a supplement to the trapper's resources for several years, and some of the men now turned more to that activity as a means of getting by. Manson and Bill began regular excursions into the marshes at night with headlights and shotguns in search of swamp rabbits, the larger species of the rodent family which brought more return on the market than their smaller cottontail cousins of the prairie region. They would usually take along about fifty shotgun shells for each of them and often return from the night's hunt with upward of one hundred rabbits between them, the hunt often being completed before midnight.

One of their favorite rabbit hunting haunts was Cove Island and the surrounding area, located near the shore of Trinity Bay and not far west of the mouth of the Trinity River. The night's kill was usually cleaned immediately after the completion of the hunt, the entrails extracted from the furry bodies before the young men retired for the night with the stars in the sky and the trees on Cove Island as their only roof. On one occasion, they were so exhausted upon the completion of their hunt that they agreed to wait until the following morning to tend to the kill. After a good night's rest on the island, they arose early the next morning and with their pocket knives began the familiar chore of gutting the rabbits. To their dismay, they found that the animals' entrails had swelled during the night to a point that made it practically impossible to cut the initial incision through the skin on the belly side without puncturing the swollen entrails, thereby ruining the animals for marketable value. With slow, tedious strokes of the knives, they managed to salvage some of the carcasses for sale, hauling them to a market in Crosby the following day where they received thirty-five cents per pair for the rabbits.

During the early 1920's, good quality raccoon hides were bringing some eight dollars on the market, a price which could have amounted to a small fortune for those days had the population of the furry, masked animals not been at such a low ebb. But, such is the character of a market based upon the concept of supply and demand. The coon population was decidedly low in most sections of the country and the nation was entering an era to be known as the "Roaring '20's" during which one of the most fashionable clothing items was the raccoon coat. As furriers scrambled to obtain their share of coon pelts in the big fur brokerage houses of New York City, the demand became greater through spirited competition, and the heavy demand trickled down to the origin of the skins themselves – the local fur trapper. Now was the time for the trapper to earn some good money, provided he could locate and catch the coons.

In 1922, Manson Clark was running a trap line for coons in the marshes southeast of a string of islands known locally as "The Ridge" on the old Joseph Lawrence Survey. Since the area was indeed behind The Ridge geographically from the settled location of the Cove community on the highland, most local folks referred to this portion of the marshlands as "back of The Ridge." Most natural landmarks of the region became tagged with that title, including a bayou known as "Back of The Ridge Bayou." (Some local people would later come to call the stream "Dunn's Bayou" due to the purchase of the land on both banks by Lindsey H. Dunn, Sr.)

To reach this area, Manson rowed his skiff across Cotton Lake to the head of Cross Bayou, the latter of which was then only a small, narrow and shallow slough which cut its way southward through the marshes to Trinity Bay. A short distance down the bayou, he secured his boat to the east bank, unloaded the traps and other necessary equipment, and began the long trek overland across the marshes to The Ridge.

Since the trip usually consumed a major part of the day, it was generally near sunset when he finally finished laying a trap line through this saltgrass region. He then camped for the night on one of the small islands of the chain that made The Ridge in order to be near his trap line at sunrise the following morning.

Running his traps one cool morning this season, he happened upon a coon caught by a foot in one of his steel traps. As he had done on so many occasions in recent years, the seventeen-year-old trapper secured the wooden club he used to strike his trapped animals on the head to effect the kill. As he raised the weapon for the strike, the coon suddenly threw both front paws before his face and covered his masked eyes. Touched by this sort of obvious fear on the part of the furry creature, Manson lowered the club to his side and took a closer look at the pitiful sight. The coon then lowered his paws back to the muddy marsh ground. Manson again raised the weapon and took aim on the dark gray head, only to have the animal repeat his eye-covering routine. "I can't hit that coon like that," Manson told himself. Suddenly, the trapper felt awful. Here, he had a nice eight dollar coon in a trap, totally at his mercy, and could not bring himself to kill the animal. The charade of the raising of the club and the covering of the eyes was repeated several times. Manson was used to the animals either fighting at him or fighting the trap in an effort to escape, and he had no problem in delivering the killing blow under such circumstances. But, this coon was different; the animal acted almost human.

Finally, Manson noticed that the coon's foot was not caught very securely in the trap. Perhaps with a little time to himself, he might manage to pull out of the contraption and go on his way. Therefore, the trapper determined to leave the coon for the time being, go ahead and run the remainder of his trap line, then return to the set, by which time he hoped the coon would have freed himself and be gone.

A couple hours later, Manson completed the running of the trap line and sloshed back through the mud to the scene he had left earlier. He was dismayed at the sight which greeted him. There, watching his return through a pair of shiny black eyes, sat the coon with the trap still fastened to his foot. The relatively unchanged scene about the set told Manson that the animal had hardly made any attempt at all to escape during his absence. It would be cruel, he thought, to leave the coon in the trap any longer. Raising his club for the decisive blow, the coon again covered his eyes, but Manson would not allow the pathetic sight to again deter him from what he had to do. Squinting his own eyes in an effort to partially blur the scene before him, Manson brought the club down hard against the animal's head. The coon fell to the muddy marsh floor and now assumed the appearance of so many other such animals Manson had had to kill during his early years on the trap line.

As the trapper released the stilled paw and reset the trap, he could still see visions of that masked face with the paws over the eyes. The thought haunted him that night as he lay in camp. He felt somewhat as if he had taken a human life, or at least the life of a faithful dog. It would be many years before Manson could approach a trap which held a coon and not have that disspiriting sight return to his mind. He would never again catch an animal which would exhibit such a nature. Manson later wrote in his journal: "I have caught many a coon, but that one was one pitiful sight that I will always wish I could have turned loose."

■   ■   ■   ■   ■   ■   ■

By the latter part of the 1920's, the muskrats were beginning to make a comeback in the marshes after their almost complete demise from the flood waters early in the decade. In 1927, their buildup was becoming evident and Manson decided to take a few traps to the marsh to determine to just what extent they had reproduced.

Bogging his way into an exceptionally low area where several 'rat beds were scattered about, he began checking a few of the "runs" to learn if they were fresh. This method involved the insertion of his hand into the shallow, covered trails at the point where they appeared on the surface. If the floor of the run felt smooth to the touch, it was a good sign that muskrats were using it frequently and keeping it open by nightly travel. Thrusting his hand into one such run, Manson immediately felt the pain of a bite on a finger. "Cottonmouth!", he thought instantly before realizing it was too cool for the snakes to be prowling about. Jerking his hand from the hole; he caught a glimpse of a muskrat with its teeth firmly embedded in his finger. Flinging his hand upward with a violent motion, he felt the rodent's teeth tear from the finger, taking a sizeable hunk of flesh as the 'rat was flung loose and hurtled skyward some twenty feet above the marsh grass. The painful, bloody cut would be a long time in healing and for twenty years afterward would subject Manson to periods of pain. The scar from the teeth of the 'rat would never completely disappear.

■   ■   ■   ■   ■   ■   ■

In 1928, Manson and Bill had been doing some alligator hunting in the marshes around Lake Charlotte, located east of the Trinity River and not far from the Chambers-Liberty county line. On one of these trips, Saylus "Sails" Elliott, a resident of the West Bay area, went along with the two Clarks on an expedition into the Lake Charlotte marshes. During the course of the excursion, they happened upon a twelve-foot-long alligator and determined to capture the reptile alive. Employing several ropes and a lot of tugging and pulling, they managed to subdue the large animal and took him back to Cove.

Now that they had a big live 'gator on their hands, the next question was what to do with him. Someone mentioned that people just might pay a nominal fee to view the creature, but such an idea was out of the question in Cove, an area where at that time alligators were more plentiful than people. Then, the thought was advanced that if they could take the 'gator farther away from the marshes where folks were not so used to seeing the reptiles, there just might be some promise in such a scheme. They had been hearing stories about thousands of people flocking into the upper east Texas region around the town of Kilgore where the great East Texas Oilfield was booming, and it was a pretty safe bet that many of those upland folks had never even seen a live alligator. That was it! They would head up through east Texas as soon as they could build a trailer in which to haul their "marsh monster."

Bill was not too inclined to make the trip, although he believed the idea had real potential. He was willing to help get things ready for the trip, but decided he would remain behind in Cove and hunt a few more alligators himself. Sails had another job he needed to hang onto and could not afford to take the time off for the journey. Manson, however, was determined to go. If they would only help him build the trailer, he would buy their "shares" in the 'gator and make the trip alone. This sounded like a good deal to everyone concerned. As things turned out, however, Manson did not have to go alone. A man from Pelly, over in Harris County, named Slim Dorsett was out of work and agreed to ride to Kilgore with Manson. It promised to be a real adventure and he figured the fun involved would make the trip more than worthwhile.

Slim was a good friend to Sails Elliott and Sails knew his friend had quite a talent with an artist's brush. It did not take much coaxing to talk Slim into painting a sign to nail to the side of the trailer for the advertisement of their new venture. His artistry resulted in a picture of a large alligator chasing a colored man, over which were painted the words, "12-Foot Alligator." With everything prepared, the men fastened the trailer to Manson's Model-T Ford and headed northward into east Texas – with a total of $3.00 in Manson's pocket.

Arriving first at the town of Henderson, they were informed that the bulk of the transient oilfield workers were concentrated about the town of Kilgore, heart of the gigantic oil boom. Driving into Kilgore, Manson saw more people than he had ever believed could live in one area. On the outskirts of town, they located a travelling carnival, its shows and gambling booths drawing large crowds every night. Manson obtained permission from someone connected with the carnival to set up his alligator exhibit on the grounds. He and Slim hurriedly brushed the red east Texas dust off the sign on the trailer and Slim quickly lettered a smaller sign displaying admission prices – ten cents for adults and five cents for children – and went into business.

In recent weeks, things had been occurring in and about the oilfield area of which Manson was unaware. The great number of rowdy oilfield workers and camp followers who had besieged the boom town recently had reached the point that local law enforcement officers were unable to handle the outlawry associated with the sudden increase in population. Makeshift saloons in those days of Prohibition provided stages for daily brawls, knifings, shootings and about every other social sin and upheaval known to man. Things had become so bad, in fact, that the Governor declared martial law in the region and sent in the Texas Rangers to round up the troublemakers. The Rangers arrived at Kilgore at about the same time Manson towed his alligator trailer into town.

On this first day of business, Manson had already taken in sixty-five cents in admission fees and the prospects were very good. Then, seemingly out of nowhere, converged the Texas Rangers. The carnival was closed when it was found to be a crooked and unlawful show in its manner of operation and the drummers working the booths and sideshows were arrested and hauled away to jail. The Rangers realized that Manson and Slim were not part of the regular travelling show and had no knowledge of its illegal operations. They were, therefore, excluded from the roundup. After everyone else had been carried away by the Rangers, Manson, Slim and the alligator were left alone on the carnival grounds.

Things had not gone at all as Manson had planned. That which a few minutes earlier had appeared to be the beginning of a prosperous business venture had now all been crushed by the Rangers' raid. His enthusiasm likewise dampened, he decided then and there that this was not the life for him. His brief flirtation with show business had made him appreciate the quiet lifestyle in Cove all the more. He had much rather hunt alligators than show them. Pulling down the admission signs, he and Slim climbed back into the car and headed southward for home.

■　■　■　■　■　■

During the late 1920's, Cove alligator hunters heard that other hunters in nearby areas had begun a process known as "pole-hunting" for the reptiles. This method involved going into the marshes with a long wooden pole to which was attached at one end a large heavy-gauge hook. The hook end of the pole was thrust into the tunnel in which lay an alligator. When the 'gator bit the hook, the men then dragged the reptile out of the hole and shot him. Most of the Cove hunters did not think very highly of this process as they knew that as long as they left alone the alligators living in holes out in the marshes, and killed only those along the bayous and sloughs, there would always be a supply of the animals available for the hunters. George and Sol Wilburn reasoned, and rightly so, that this manner of hunting would eventually wipe out the alligator population, or at least reduce it to such a low number that hunting the reptiles for their marketable hides would no longer be worthwhile. If this practice was going to be allowed, they decided they might as well get their share while there were still plenty of the animals to be had. Their primary hunting ground became the Mayes Marsh on the east side of Old River Lake, where they worked to try to average a kill of ten 'gators per day.

Manson also decided to try his hand at this new form of alligator hunting. It was a tough, tiresome, back-breaking way to make a living. Equipment necessary for this form of hunting often presented transportation problems in travelling on foot through the marshes. The hook pole was a cumbersome wooden pole some twenty feet long and two inches in diameter, with a two-pronged hook on one end which Manson had had fashioned from an automobile spring. He also carried what he termed as a "progue pole", an eight- foot-long metal rod about 3/8" in diameter, slightly pointed on one end and with a small wooden handle fastened to the other end. This device was used to push down through the muddy earth of the marsh directly above the tunnel of an alligator's lair, locate the reptile, and tickle him on the back. This process usually caused the 'gator to exit the tunnel to locate the source of the disturbance whereupon a well placed bullet was usually awaiting the 'gator. Other equipment was a hatchet which Manson had learned from previous experience to have handy to chop supposedly dead alligators in the back of the head in the event they were only "playing possum" when he pulled them from the muddy pit by hand. The usual skinning knife was attached to his belt and a flat pint whiskey bottle filled with drinking water, a most important element in the hot summer marsh excursions, rested in his rear pocket.

By this time, Manson had stopped carrying a shotgun as a means of taking the reptiles. His weapon now was a single-shot .22 caliber rifle, considerably lighter in weight than the shotgun and easier to carry in the marshes. He had found that a .22 caliber long rifle hollow point bullet would kill the largest alligators in the marshes if the shot was placed with deadly accuracy to send the bullet into the small brain of the reptile.

Upon killing an alligator in the marsh during a pole-hunting excursion, it was necessary to drag the 'gator out of the watery hole and onto the marshy bank to proceed with the skinning process then and there. The heavy hide of the 'gator removed from the carcass, it was placed in a tow sack for carrying, adding yet additional weight to the already physically burdened hunter.

Manson often received tips from friends about large populations of alligators in distant areas. If he considered the information to be reliable, he would often take a trip to the described area to check it out for himself. It did not take many "wild goose chases" to learn that people unaccustomed to being around large concentrations of alligators might see a pair of the reptiles while on a fishing trip and later report to him that the 'gators were as "thick as hair" in that location. Sometimes, however, such reports proved to be quite accurate.

In 1928, Manson went on such an expedition down the coast to Matagorda County where he hoped to hunt the swamps near Bay City. Sixteen-year-old Charles Joseph, Jr., a friend and neighbor whose parents operated Joseph's Store at Cove, accompanied Manson on this trip. Arriving at the edge of the swamp in the late morning, the pair hurriedly secured a dinner meal and proceeded into the lowlands to see what they could find in the way of alligators. Bogging their way along some sloughs in the swamp, which are often used by alligators in travelling from one den to another, they soon became aware of the tremendous number of poisonous snakes which inhabited

41

this swamp, most of which were cottonmouth moccasins. Both Manson and Charles were familiar with these ugly, ill-tempered creatures whose venom is every bit as deadly as that of the diamondback rattlesnake. Unlike the rattler, the cottonmouth gives the intruder into his domain no warning before striking. The two young men soon found themselves watching as closely for cottonmouths as for alligator sign.

Manson and Charles killed seventeen medium-to-large sized 'gators during the afternoon before deciding to leave the swamp for the day and head back to camp. While working at one 'gator den, they became party to an experience which Manson had never had occur before in his years of hunting the marshes. Having pushed the hookpole into a tunnel in an effort to extract its inhabitant from the lair, the familiar jerk on the pole told the hunters the 'gator had taken the hook far back into the depths of the tunnel. Both Manson and Charles took a firm grip on the pole and began tugging. Judging from the amount of resistance they encountered, it was believed that an alligator of some ten to twelve feet in length was on the double-pronged hook. Inches at a time, they laboriously brought the end of the pole to the surface. As the hook emerged, and the usual fighting and splashing commenced in the pit, they realized they had two 'gators hooked, one on either prong, each about five feet in length. Never again in all his years of hunting the marsh denizens would Manson see this act repeated.

Back home in Cove, the Trinity River went on a rampage during the spring and early summer of 1929, following a series of heavy spring rains throughout east Texas. As the tremendous volume of water rushed southward toward Trinity Bay, it spread out over the lowlands of central Chambers County and inundated the marshes below Cove. With the water over the marshes, it became possible to navigate a rowboat over most of what was usually boggy marshland. Manson took advantage of the situation and went after alligators on night hunting expeditions. During the month of June that year, he killed 228 alligators. Those measuring between seven and twelve feet in length brought a maximum price of $4.50 each.

One night during the late 1920's, one of Zack Maley's sons, Guy, accompanied Manson on a hunt for alligators in the lower reaches of Shell Bayou, a small stream which entered the marshes from the bay just west of the mouth of Cross Bayou. At that time, Shell Bayou terminated a short distance north of its mouth at a large pond, although in later years it would wash through north of the pond to a confluence with Cross Bayou.

Emerging onto Trinity Bay from Cross Bayou, they turned the twelve-foot skiff westward along the bayshore until they reached the entrance to Shell Bayou. Manson had brought along his French harp in case no alligators were to be found. In such an eventuality, they could at least strike up a few old traditional tunes on the route back home. As they quietly entered the mouth of the little stream, he placed the instrument on the front seat of the boat and prepared to get down to business.

Not far up the bayou, they spotted the bright red eye of a 'gator, shot the reptile, and went through the familiar task of dragging the eight-foot-long beast into the boat, allowing him to sprawl lifelessly in the floor of the skiff. Proceeding farther up the stream, they paid little attention to, the occasional squirming of the alligator in the boat as the animals often go through such involuntary movements due to postmortem nerve action within their bodies.

Suddenly, the 'gator came to life, having apparently been only stunned by the bullet. Raising his head from the floor of the skiff, he opened his mouth wide enough to reveal jaws full of uneven teeth, and furiously slapped the side of the boat with his heavy tail. Exhaling noisily through the nose, a common manner in the exhibition of displeasure by the reptiles, the 'gator went on a virtual rampage, biting at everything in sight and flailing the massive tail from side to side. Trapped in the boat with the 'gator in the middle of the bayou, Manson and Guy each prepared to abandon the craft if necessary. Manson perched himself on the precarious edge of one side of the boat while Guy assumed a similar position on the other gunwale. Between them, they watched as the enraged 'gator literally "cleaned the decks."

The beast lunged toward the stern of the skiff. His first obstacle, the wooden rear seat, he caught between his powerful jaws and snapped in half, clearing out the rear section of the boat. The hunters hoped the 'gator would fling himself over the stern of the boat and disappear into the muddy waters of the bayou. Upon reaching the stern, however, he doubled his wiry body into the shape of a horseshoe, spun around in the skiff, and headed for the bow. On this return trip through the boat, the beast bit out the two remaining seats. As he planted his teeth firmly into the bow seat, Manson's French harp fell to the floor of the boat. Back and forth through the boat the 'gator lurched and raged, with the two hunters still perched on either side, not unlike mockingbirds on a barbed wire fence.

Guy managed to reach a section of one of the broken boat seats the alligator had cleared from his path. As the animal passed by on a return trip through the vessel, Guy raised the plank and brought it down swiftly in an attempt to strike the beast behind the head. The 'gator's erratic movements caused Guy's aim to go wild, and the sharp corner of the board came down hard against the floor of the boat, gouging a deep dent into one of the cypress planks of which the boat was constructed. As the reptile recoiled and made another pass by them, Guy again brought the makeshift weapon down. This time the board found its mark, crashing into the alligator's head just behind the skull. Immediately, the 'gator went limp, but both hunters knew he was only stunned and would soon renew the attack. Manson rapidly paddled the boat to the bayou bank where they dragged the 'gator onto the marshy ground and fired a well-aimed bullet into the brain of the reptile.

Realizing the dangerous position they had been in only minutes before and thankful now to have come out of it as well as they had, the two hunters observed their partially wrecked boat. Not a seat or any other obstacle remained in the craft. Laying on the floor near the bow was Manson's French harp. "When that 'gator first headed for the bow of the boat," Guy quipped to Manson, "I thought he was just wanting to play a tune on your French harp!" The two had to laugh at Guy's statement in the quiet aftermath of what could have been a tragic situation.

■　■　■　■　■　■　■

On the horizon loomed worldwide economic disaster. While most of the people of tiny Cove, Texas knew little about national or international financial matters, they did realize that the decade of the 1920's had brought good times. On January 23, 1926, Manson had married Miss Comelia Fannett of Old River community. On June 23, 1927, they had a daughter whom they named Gloria Gertrude. In late 1929, as the economic structure of the nation began to collapse, another child was on the way. Born January 31, 1930, the second daughter was named Freda Marie. With a growing family, Manson worked even harder and longer hours in the marshes to provide for those under his care.

During his off seasons between hunting, trapping and fishing, Manson worked for the Pure Oil Company which, during the waning months of the 1920's, had brought in an oilfield in the marshes near Lost Lake. Suddenly, there was a demand for workers in the marshy oilfield. Several of the available men in Cove answered the call for the jobs, which paid $4.25 per day.

The company established its docks on the west side of Old River, a short distance north of its confluence with the north end of Old River Lake. Quincy Icet of Cove became boat captain and hauled crews and equipment back and forth from the docks to the work site near Lost Lake. The workers, however, had to physically carry and roll the heavy drill pipe across the stretch of marsh between Old River and Lost River in some of the most gruelling work ever devised by man. Manson became a "roughneck" and soon began assuming the job of "working derrick" which required him to scale the drilling rig to the topmost platform from which he was to center the drill pipe for its journey into the bowels of the earth below, probing for the "black gold." This vantage point atop the rig also gave him an opportunity to visibly scan the marshes in all directions for concentrations of ducks on a nearby pond, or a buildup of muskrat beds in a particular sector, or even likely alligator dens.

When weather conditions were right, Manson was usually absent from the oilfield work. At such times he could generally be found alone in the marshes hunting 'gators or trapping 'rats. Now and then, the men on the drilling rig set their minds to having a duck dinner, whereupon the man in charge would often send Manson into the marshes with his shotgun to secure the necessary meat for the feast, a task from which he never balked. Due to his propensity for the marsh life, some of the men good-naturedly began calling Manson "Alligator," a nickname which would stick with him for many years.

Three months after the discovery of oil at Lost Lake, the nation as a whole was plunged into the worst economic crisis in its history. On October 29, 1929, the national stock market crashed. Loud was the fall of the American economy. The Pure Oil Company, often known locally as simply "The Pure," continued to work men in the Lost Lake field for quite some time after the onset of the Great Depression, as was the case in several other fledgling oilfields in Texas, thereby staving off the realities of the times in this region for a couple years. However, the inevitable decline was certain to encompass even the booming oil industry.

One final hunt of the decade would signal the end of the "Roaring '20's" for Manson Clark. Johnny Roberts, son of local commercial fisherman Charley Roberts, had told Manson about an area near the mouth of the San Bernard River, in southwestern Brazoria County, where the coons were known to be "as thick as hair." In the bottomlands southwest of the town of Freeport was a forbidding stretch of swampland known locally as "The Cowtrap," so styled due to the great number of cattle and other livestock claimed by the boggy morass throughout the years. Manson was determined to try his luck with the raccoons of this so-called Cowtrap.

Manson and his younger brother, Vane, left Cove and traveled southwestward to Angleton, and then on to the town of West Columbia, near the bank of the San Bernard. South of the town they rented a boat from a fisherman on the river, leaving Manson's car in his charge until they should return. Moving several miles downstream, they encountered a heavy fog cloud which almost totally obscured the river banks on both sides of the stream. Night having set in, they strained their eyes to make out the vision of any obstacle in their front and soon saw a houseboat tied up against the river bank. Pulling alongside the houseboat, they found an old fisherman who lived on the river and was ready for visitors, complete with coffee and a long line of conversation. They asked him how they might reach The Cowtrap, and he obliged by giving them detailed instructions as to how far down the river to travel and which sloughs to take to the place. They mentioned to him that they had noticed an unusually large number of rattlesnakes along the banks of the river at points where they had put ashore during this unseasonably warm December night. "Yeah," the old man replied, "they's lots o'rattlers hereabouts, but I ain't as skeered o' them as I am o' them cottonmouths they got over 'bout the mouth of the Trinity River." Manson and Vane told the fisherman that that was where they had come from. "Y'all better watch them snakes," the talkative old man told the brothers. "The rattlers'll warn ya when ya git too close to 'em, but them cottonmouths will jist lay there and wait fer ya to come in strikin' range. And they ever bit as deadly as these rattlers." Manson and Vane could not argue with the point made by the fisherman and they all agreed that it was just whatever a man was used to that really made the difference in his fear of a particular creature. Thanking the old man for his hospitality, the pair headed farther down the river.

The fog finally became so thick as they drew nearer the mouth of the river that they decided they might never find The Cowtrap tonight. They agreed to put ashore where they were now and see if they might find any coons in the immediate vicinity. They found no coons, but did find that the polecats were plentiful so decided to try to pay for their trip with the furs of some of the smelly creatures. They had not walked far from the boat when they heard the unmistakable rattling of a snake. Looking under a bush where the sound seemed to be coming from, they quickly discovered the reptile was hidden beneath some brush in the opposite direction. Still a second rattler was soon detected with the sound likewise being difficult to determine as to the direction.

Killing both these rattlesnakes, as well as a couple skunks, they decided there was not much hope for a successful coon hunt in the fog tonight anyhow, and headed back toward the boat. Skinning the polecats, they also decided to remove the skins and rattlers from the snakes. After all, the decorative covering of a rattlesnake was something that not many folks in Cove had ever seen.

As Manson and Vane boarded the skiff for the trip back upriver, a chilling northerly wind suddenly cut through the midnight darkness, sending a shiver over the young men. As they moved northward back upstream, the wind increased in intensity and frigidity until they were certain the temperature must be well below the freezing mark. At least, the strong north wind had blown the fog away and they now had no trouble in visually finding their way back up the San Bernard. It would be several hours before they reached the landing where they had rented the boat and had left Manson's car. Manson now feared that the radiator in the vehicle would be frozen and ruptured before they could return, stranding them in the Brazoria County river bottoms. Upon finally reaching the landing, they were relieved to learn that the man from whom they had rented the skiff had recognized such a possibility and had drained the water from the radiator, thereby averting such a mishap.

Relieved to find the car in good condition upon their return, they cranked the car engine into motion, refilled the radiator with water, and began the long trek back home. Most of the roads over which they had traveled from Cove to Brazoria County had been muddy, rut-strewn trails in which it was necessary to keep the wheels of the vehicle in the ruts formed earlier by automobile traffic. Now, on their return trip, they found that the mud had literally frozen on the surface of the roads and they were able to drive upon the upper layer of the mud and ice practically all the way home to Cove.

This trip had certainly proven to be a miscarriage of a hunt. They had not been able to locate The Cowtrap, the real object of their trip, had not seen a coon, and brought back with them only a couple of polecat and rattlesnake skins. It was, perhaps, a hunt prophetic in nature of times to come during the next decade.

• CHAPTER IV •

THE 1930's

Muskrats had begun to make quite a comeback in the Cove marshes by 1930, after having been practically wiped out by high water a decade ago. However, with the prevailing Depression era economics being what they were, there was little financial comfort to be realized from the fur trapping business. Fur is a luxury item and during hard times such products are likely to be left in the stores as consumers predictably spend their limited income on food and other necessities of life. Reflecting the downswing in the American fur market, the trapper soon found that he could expect only some 25¢ for large, top quality muskrat fur. This was the case in southeast Texas despite the fact that the fur on muskrats found in Chambers and Jefferson counties in Texas is widely recognized as the finest quality of muskrat fur available anywhere. This same luxury problem was evidenced in the market for alligator hides as the price for large 'gator skins dropped to $2.25 each, regardless of the length of the reptile, reflecting a fifty percent decrease from the price offered during the summer of 1929.

One hot summer day during the early 1930's, Clarence Porter, a resident of the Old River community, was on his way to work at the Lost Lake Oilfield, and chanced to pass Manson on the way, the latter struggling with a long hook pole deep in a marshy alligator tunnel. The area was the Icet Marsh, not far from the oilfield. Manson had a large 'gator on the hook and was having quite some difficulty in extracting the reptile from the tunnel. Seeing Clarence passing at a distance, the hunter called to him to send him some help to pull the alligator from the hole. Arriving at the worksite, Clarence approached one of the foremen and told him Manson needed some help with something out in the marsh. The man was acquainted with Manson, and was one of those who called him by the nickname of "Alligator."

The man headed out into the marsh to assist his former drilling rig employee. At the 'gator pit the man hesitated a bit when he saw what Manson was up to, but when the hunter asked him to grasp the pole and help him pull the alligator out, the man obliged. With the additional force on the pole, the 'gator began to lose his hold on the floor of the tunnel deep in the earth and the men began to step backward with the pole as the reptile gave way. Suddenly, the hook emerged from the hole and with it came the savage fighting of the 'gator on the hook. The powerful tail of the reptile slapped furiously, sending mud and water in all directions. Manson's assistant, thinking the alligator had released his grip on the hook and was coming after them, turned loose of the pole and headed for the open marshes in a run, at least as rapidly as was possible in the boggy terrain. Manson managed to hold the hook pole with one hand and take his rifle with the other to make a killing shot at the animal. The oilfield boss stood watching at a short, but safe distance away. When the man returned to the drilling rig, he told Clarence never to ask him to go into the marsh to help Manson with another gator.

■　■　■　■　■　■　■

As economic depression over the country had finally begun to take a firm grip in southeast Texas, Manson decided to attempt to add some sort of supplement to the family coffers by putting in a cotton crop. It had been several years since he had done any farming and really had little equipment for the work. Without any work animals of his own (he had declared years ago he never wanted to handle another cow, horse or mule), he borrowed a pair of mules from his neighbor, Linzie Griffith. Harnessing the team one morning and following them to the field, he recalled how he and Bill, as boys, used to be convinced that the farm animals would hatch plots between themselves to foil the noble intentions of those responsible for working them. If he thought today that such was just a silly boyhood theory, he was about to have the youthful idea driven home to him as a matter of fact.

Approaching an open gap in the barbed wire fence which enclosed the field, Manson slapped the rumps of the animals with the harness strap and urged them through the opening. He noticed the mules turn their heads toward each other and could not help but wonder if they might be cooking up some sort of devious plan. Then, just as the animals started through the opening in the fence, they suddenly wheeled about in a northerly direction, one of them on either side of the fence, and broke into a wild run along the jagged strands of the barbed wire. "Whoa, whoa!," Manson yelled as he attempted to gain a foothold in the black gumbo dirt along the fence row. Every time he yelled at the animals, they seemed to turn on more energy. Thoughts of anger and of boyhood days on the farm raced through his mind. "It's just the meanness in them," he reasoned. "They would run themselves to death to make life miserable for someone else!"

As fence posts snapped under the onslaught of the harness straps connecting the two mules, the barbs on the wire began to cut into Manson's arms and sides as he realized that the animals were totally out of control. Unable to hold out any longer, he finally released his grip on the lines and fell flat into the dirt beside the fence. The mules continued their wild race for a short distance more, then suddenly stopped about fifty yards ahead of Manson's prone position. Manson raised himself from the dirt and walked toward the animals while examining his cuts and bruises. The harness was a shambles, the fence posts and wire having cut portions out of the straps as the crazed beasts made their senseless run. Due to the position of one mule being on either side of the fence, he had to release them from the harness which connected them across the strands of wire. As anger increased within him, he became convinced that what he and Bill had held as a theory about farm animals was, in reality, a fact. Years later, Manson would recall the incident. "If I had had a gun with me that day, I would have had to pay Linzie for his mules, because I would have killed them both right there. If anything ever needed killing, it was those two mules." As he finally managed to release the mules from the harness and led them away from the fence, the thought kept recurring in his mind, "Oh, if they were only mine......."

■ ■ ■ ■ ■ ■ ■

With the price of alligator hides depressed to an all time low during the early 1930's, Manson turned to another form of nighttime work as a supplement to his income by wading the shallow waters along the Trinity Bay shoreline in search of flounder fish. The process was simple. A kerosene lantern was carried in one hand to illuminate the water directly ahead in order to spot the dark outline of the broad, flat fish lying on the sandy bay floor. A flounder "gig" was employed to stab the fish. The gig consisted merely of a wooden pole some four feet in length and very similar to that of a broom handle, with a pointed metal rod, of some 1/4" in diameter, firmly embedded in one end of the pole.

Manson and Bill did quite a bit of floundering during the early thirties near the mouths of Cove, Dunn and Long Island bayous. Their catch varied greatly, ranging from some ten flounders in less than desirable conditions upward to ninety when wind and water conditions were favorable. Little or no breeze on the bay provided the best floundering conditions, because too much wave action tended to make the water muddy, thereby decreasing the chances of seeing any flounders in the glow of the lantern's light. They sold the fish for twelve cents per pound and, as Manson later wrote, "We didn't make much money, but we lived."

One night a friend of Bill's went along with them for a floundering trip in the bay. As was their usual custom, the three men spread out some thirty to forty feet apart, each with a lantern and gig, and began their night's work. The new man was very excited about the whole matter as he had never been floundering before. The Clark brothers had told him that when he gigged a flounder, he must hold it down to the bay bottom with the gig until it could be secured by his hand and placed on a fish stringer. As the three men waded along, Manson and Bill routinely gigged a flounder now and then but it took the novice some little while to become accustomed to what he was looking for in the water in his path. Finally, he saw a flounder and thrust his gig through the fish. "I've got one!" he yelled to Bill, to which the latter replied, "Hold him down." "He's jumpin' around!" the man advised, and Bill again told him to "Hold him down." Each time Bill told the man to hold the flounder down, he pushed the gig farther through the fish, finally burying the wooden handle of the gig through the dark figure and some two feet deep into the bay floor. By the time Bill and Manson reached the man's location to show him how to retrieve the flounder, no more than twelve inches of the gig handle still protruded above the fish, and the man was still pushing! He was determined that his flounder not get away.

■ ■ ■ ■ ■ ■ ■

In the depth of the Depression era, Manson continued to work the marshes and bay, by both day and night, to provide for his family. His first marriage having gone awry, he had married Miss Myra Maley, one of Joseph Maley's daughters, on January 21, 1933. He also retained legal custody of his two daughters, Gloria and Freda.

Not long after his second entry into matrimony, he and Owen Maley, eldest son of Zack Maley, decided to conduct an alligator hunt in Robinson Bayou, a stream which they had been told had a considerable number of 'gators. It was a long run by boat to the bayou. In order to reach the bayou, they had to cross Trinity Bay, round the protrusion of land known as Smith Point in extreme southern Chambers County, and travel eastward on East Bay to the mouth of Robinson Bayou. The stream itself was "the crookedest bayou I have ever seen," Manson later revealed. It was but a short distance northward through the marshes to where the stream headed at Robinson Lake, but the bayou covered several miles in length through its endless curves and bends.

Making the trip in Manson's inboard Cushman rig, he and Owen crossed Trinity Bay to Smith Point and entered East Bay without incident. Arriving at the mouth of Robinson Bayou, they awaited the darkness and then began their night's hunt. Disappointment was in store for them on this expedition, however. Either someone else had already been hunting the alligators in the bayou and took a heavy toll on them or they had received some bad information about the number of alligators in Robinson Bayou. At any rate, they had spent two days and nights on the trip, not to mention the gasoline the one-cylinder engine had consumed, and had not even paid expenses with their kill. They decided to leave the area and begin the long trip back across Trinity Bay toward Cove.

Back on the waters of East Bay, a rare, breezy norther had moved through the region. The weather was still warm, but the wind kept them navigating as near the north shore of the bay as the water level would permit. Arriving at Smith Point, they were running noticeably low on fuel, so decided to put in at the Point and purchase some gasoline at a small store in the fishing village located there. Again, they were disappointed to learn that the store was out of its supply of gasoline. Realizing they did not have enough fuel for the trip back to Cove, or even to run up the east shore of Trinity Bay to Anahuac, they found themselves in a predicament for which no ready solution was in sight. A. E. "Buddy" Whitehead, a nearby property owner and oilfield maintenance man, happened by the store while Manson and Owen were there and offered to drive to his home, a few miles east of Smith Point, and secure them a supply of gasoline. True to his word, Whitehead soon arrived back at the Point with a five-gallon can of fuel, which was poured into the boat engine. When Manson attempted to pay the man for the gasoline and his assistance, Whitehead would accept no money. It was not often that he had an opportunity to help any strangers in the isolated Point area and he was just glad to be of aid to them. As Manson and Owen left the Point, they knew they would never forget the benevolence of this kind man.

Camping for the night on one of the Vingt-et-Un Islands just off Smith Point, they made their way the next morning in a northerly direction, paralleling the east shore of Trinity Bay. The light summer norther was still breezy and they knew the waters on the open bay would be rough. Presently arriving at the mouth of little Lone Oak Bayou by darkness that evening, Manson suggested they check it out for alligators. This proved to be a wise decision as they killed a number of the reptiles along this stream, enough at least to pay for their trip.

After almost a week away from home, Manson and Owen finally arrived back at Cove. Their families and neighbors had been greatly concerned for their safety as it had been learned during their absence that some of the landowners in the region to which they had journeyed had been shooting trespassers in the marshes. The two Cove men explained that no one would have had any reason to shoot them, because they had spent their time in the boat and had not trespassed on anyone's property. The only meeting they had had with one of the landowners in the region had been a pleasant one, they explained, as they related to their neighbors the aid rendered to them by Buddy Whitehead at Smith Point.

■ ■ ■ ■ ■ ■ ■

Through the years, the muskrats had continued their peculiar manner of living, which amounted to reducing their population during years when conditions were not exactly to their liking, then rebuilding their numbers during better times. During the winter of 1932-33, the 'rats had begun to build up again in number and Manson took some traps to the marshes to catch a few of them for an examination of the quality of the fur. He found the fur to be in good condition, but when the time came to sell the pelts it was evident just how drastically the depression was affecting the fur market. Large, top quality muskrat furs that year brought only 25¢ each. By the winter of 1933-34, the price had recovered to between 40¢ and 70¢ for the best furs. 'Rats caught during the 1934-35 season brought about 80¢ each by the end of the season, which was no little sum of income during the Depression era. Matters were also helped along that winter by the fact that good weather conditions had provided the muskrats with a good breeding year, thereby increasing their population. Manson caught some 1,300 'rats that winter as conditions began to look somewhat more favorable in all quarters.

■ ■ ■ ■ ■ ■ ■

For three weeks after his marriage to Myra, Manson had been renting a house in Cove for his wife, two daughters, and himself. Desiring a place of his own, he approached his father, William, with the notion of purchasing an old shotgun house near the eastern corner of the Clark property in which William once housed his hired cotton pickers. Various newly wed couples had rented the house from William during recent years until they were able to provide their own dwelling. Bennie and Hazel Maley had been the most recent to rent the building and it was now vacant. The price for settling the real estate deal between William and his son was $125.00, payment for the house and an acre of land. When Manson and his family moved into the old house, the only furniture inside was a bed and a cane-bottomed, straight-backed chair. Other items would be added as income from the marshes allowed, and additional rooms would be built. In 1937, Myra gave birth to a daughter whom they named Florrie Gene, but the baby died only hours after birth and was buried near the Joe Maley home. Manson's mother, Mrs. Florence (Smith) Clark, had died two years earlier and the family had yet hardly gotten over this loss.

■　■　■　■　■　■　■

In the month of March, the weather had turned off very spring-like for so early in the year. Green vegetation was showing itself everywhere in the marshes and mosquitoes were already becoming a nuisance. March 15 was the last legal day of the muskrat season and it was just as well, because the weather was rapidly turning too warm to continue trapping. Manson was out on his last trapping day of the season, having picked up his last fifty-one traps with them across his shoulder in a towsack. Bogging his way out of the Lawrence Marsh, south of Cotton Lake, he picked his way along the edge of a mucky slough surrounded by tall seacane. Coming to a point where the slough widened to some fifteen feet in diameter, he recognized the location as the probable site of an alligator den, and tried to adjust his eyes to spot the dark mouth of a tunnel into the ground just below the surface of the water. Suddenly, the soupy floor gave way beneath his feet and he slid downward into chest deep mud and water. What a mess! He removed the sack of traps from his shoulder and heaved the weight into the seacane on the slough bank.

Aware that he might be standing in the muddy entrance to the alligator tunnel, Manson decided he had better get out of his predicament quickly before the ugly inhabitant of the den stirred itself and came crawling out of the tunnel to find what was causing the disturbance. Then, the marshman caught a glimpse of something moving slowly toward him from the other side of the small pond, entering the pit from the narrow neck of the slough. The bony, black head gave evidence that the 'gator was about eight feet in length. The reptile was bound for the security of its tunnel, and there was Manson, bogged down at the entrance.

The alligator stopped its advance in the center of the pond, staring at the human intruder as if in an effort to hypnotize him. Manson thought quickly. Spring and warm weather had come earlier than usual this year, causing the alligators to stir from their winter hibernation at an earlier date. They were on the prowl for food to fill their empty stomachs, not having received any nourishment since last October when they entered the tunnels for the winter sleep. Was Manson going to be this 'gator's first spring meal?

Manson knew his best chance was to remain motionless to the sight of the reptile. The alligator's eyesight is not particularly sharp and he tends to rely to a great extent on the movements of his prey to make a target for his killing attack.

As Manson stood in the oily-smelling muck, barely allowing himself the luxury of breathing, he remembered that he did not even have his pistol strapped to his side. He had dropped the weapon in the mud yesterday while picking up part of his trapline and this morning had left it dismantled at camp to allow the parts to dry. Normally, he carried it with him on the trapline during warm days to shoot cottonmouths which raised their ugly heads in his path. Even if he had brought it with him today, it would be at his side, now some two feet deep in the mud, and would be useless.

As he stood returning the stare from the creature across the pit, something else caught his eye. A cottonmouth moccasin silently swam across the pond, its hideous black body following an even more grotesque, diamond-shaped head, weaving its way toward him. "What else is going to come out of that slough?" Manson wondered as he purposely froze his muscles in the face of this new threat. Fearful of turning his head, lest he attract the attention of either of the creatures, Manson now moved only his eyes to follow the course of the snake. The cottonmouth silently swam beside him and slithered its way out onto the marshy bank of the pit and into the seacane. With this temporary threat out of the way, Manson could now turn his attention back to the alligator.

As man and beast glared at each other, separated only by some fifteen feet of muddy water, the man knew that in this case the beast had the upper hand. Suddenly, the black head again began an advance toward Manson, slowly and noiselessly. "Is he coming for me, or for his tunnel?" the trapper wondered. Now, less than ten feet away, Manson determined that if the 'gator came within arm length of him, he could not risk allowing the reptile to make the first move. The alligator is as quick as lightning in his own watery habitat, and if the 'gator made a rapid bolt at him with those powerful jaws, he would have no chance whatsoever to subdue the animal. Onward the 'gator came, only its head visible upon the surface of the water. Five feet away ..... then three .....

Manson could no longer depend upon the possibility that the alligator might swim by him and enter the tunnel. Suddenly, the trapper lashed out with his bare hands and caught the reptile around the mouth. The 'gator went wild with surprise and anger. The silence of the ancient marshlands was rudely broken by the sounds of combat between the adversaries. The man knew only that he had to maintain his grip on those jaws while at the same time keeping clear of the backbreaking tail of the alligator, now throwing mud and water like so many bullets through the thick stand of seacane surrounding them. Manson had held many other smaller 'gators by the jaws in past years while applying a blow to the back of their heads with a hatchet, but he had learned from experience that although it is possible to hold the jaws shut on an alligator of any size, a man cannot control the twisting, slashing body movements of a 'gator of more than six feet in length. If he only had his hatchet now! But, he never carried that weapon except when actually hunting alligators, and this excursion had not begun as a 'gator hunt.

The reptile, unable to wrest his snout free from the marshman's viselike grip, tried another tactic. Backing himself around to a point where his tail reached the edge of the pit, the alligator began backing out of the water onto the marshy ground. As he slowly continued his reverse movement, Manson held to his grip on the bony mouth and felt his own body being pulled from the mud. Farther and farther the reptile backed his way into the seacane, dragging the trapper from the mud and onto the bank with him.

Manson knew he was going to have to do something to break this stalemate very soon. His hands and arms were now rapidly growing weary from the incessant strain. Yet, he also knew that his options did not include releasing his grip from the alligator's jaws while the animal remained alive.

He had neither his pistol nor his hatchet. The one tool he did have, which might conceivably be converted into a weapon, was his pocket knife which he carried to skin the muskrats he took from his traps. Carefully securing a tighter grip on the 'gator's mouth with his left hand, Manson turned loose with his right hand and thrust it into his mud-filled pants pocket and brought the knife out. Through the years, he had learned to open the blade of a pocket knife with the fingers of one hand, but the mud on the knife on this occasion made the operation quite tedious. As he fumbled with the knife and the blade began to open, blood appeared from cuts inflicted in his fingers by the sharp steel. But, he had more important matters to consider now than cut fingers. Finally, the blade reached a point in its spring mechanism to cause it to fly open. Now, he was ready for the kill.

Raising the weapon into the air, its steel point aimed downward, the bone-weary man used what seemed to be his final burst of energy. While maintaining his left hand grip on the alligator's mouth, Manson lunged forward slightly and brought the knife down hard just behind the skull portion of the animal's head, burying the blade deep into the alligator's tiny brain. The 'gator responded with a violent writhe of the powerful body, then went limp. It was over. The mighty reptile lay sprawled lifeless before the marshman. Slowly releasing his left hand from the jaws of the alligator, Manson felt the sudden pains of muscle contraction in his hand and lower arm. Totally exhausted, he lay on the muddy marsh ground for an undetermined amount of time. Man and beast lay face to face.

■ ■ ■ ■ ■ ■ ■

The introduction of the outboard gasoline engine had brought about the most profound change in the mode of marsh transportation to date. Closely following the outboard had come the inboard engine. This still more convenient means of navigation signaled the entry of yet another form of livelihood for some Cove men. Ben Hill was probably the first Cove resident to take to Trinity Bay during the 1930's, and drag a trawl in the wake of his boat to sack up catches of shrimp. Ben was a son of lifelong seaman Eli Hill, who for most of his adult life had run freight boats from Cove to Galveston.

Viewing this new venture as a good supplement to his usual summertime activity of alligator hunting, Manson joined Ben on the open waters of the bay in quest of the little spear-faced crustacean. In those pioneer days of shrimping on Trinity Bay, Ben and Manson were often the only two people in sight over the large expanse of water, with the exception of an occasional fisherman running a trotline in the shallow waters nearer the bayshore.

■ ■ ■ ■ ■ ■ ■

While the cottonmouth moccasin has generally been considered as the most dangerous threat to marshmen in their swampy pursuits, especially during the warmer seasons of the year, venomous snakes did not have a monopoly on matters which could result in disastrous consequences in the lowlands. Herds of cattle grazing the heavily vegetated marshes sometimes gave the trappers and hunters reason to wish they were back in the security of their homes. Some such animals which tended to remain within the areas of the marsh rarely intruded upon by man were often not more than a step removed from the wild nature of the alligator and the wolf. The cattle subsisted well on the grasses and had no natural enemies in their marsh environment other than the previously mentioned snakes and occasional hurricanes which inundated the swamps and thinned the herds. It has been estimated that probably only about one cow out of a hundred is disposed to show serious "fight," and then usually when she has a calf to protect. That number escalates drastically when applied to the bulls, and cattlemen usually tended to put the most dangerous males in the marsh rather than keep them in high land pastures where their exposure to humans might be more likely.

Manson's father, William, was one of those who had had a close call with such a bovine in about 1900. A farmer by occupation and not one who took up the marsh life on a full time basis, William nevertheless, like most Cove men, occasionally enjoyed a good hunt in the lowlands. On this day, he had spotted a pond teeming with pintail ducks in the marsh. With no seacane in the area to conceal his movement, he had decided to assume a prone position in the surrounding salt grass and attempt to crawl up to a point within shooting range of the pond, being careful not to plug his double-barreled shotgun with mud in the process. Forgetting everything else around him in his slow slither across the open space, his first indication that he was not alone came when he heard the snort of an animal directly behind him. Stopping to glance back over his shoulder, he saw a large brindled bull peering down at him as if puzzled by the strange sight he had encountered in his domain. William immediately recognized the animal as one he had heard other hunters warn of that was always ready for a fight. He realized he had only one option, that being to deliver the first blow before the bull attacked. Quickly rolling over onto his back, William pointed his gun directly into the bull's face at point-blank range, and pulled both triggers. The simultaneous shot from both barrels knocked the animal to his knees amid a loud bellow. The angle of the shot literally peeled the hide from the bull's face. The animal turned and ran away, but would live to fight again. From that day forward, however, his fury would be directed at sounds he heard in the marshes, the double gunshot load having blinded him. As might be expected, the shot had scared the ducks from the pond, but had allowed William to escape back to his boat on a nearby bayou.

When Manson began spending more and more time in the marshes as a teenager, William told him about his escapade with the bull some twenty years before and warned him to keep an eye out for cottonmouths and semi-wild marsh cattle. Occasionally coming across small herds of cattle in the marsh, Manson developed a technique with which he became somewhat comfortable in scaring the animals away from his path. He would stop and stand silently and motionless for a minute or two as he faced the cows which appeared to be trying to figure out what he was. Then he would suddenly throw his hands above his head, "tryin' to look as big and mean as I could," and growl or yell as loudly as his usually soft voice would allow. Invariably, the animals would turn and run in the opposite direction as rapidly as possible in the boggy terrain. This method worked quite well for some time. However, as in the case of humans, not all members of the bovine kingdom were cut from the same cloth.

One morning in the late 1930s, Manson was running muskrat traps in the salt grass marsh east of Rabbit Bayou, a small stream that emptied into Trinity Bay to the west of Cove Bayou. Under a crisp, clear sky, he had walked several hundred yards from his skiff on the bayou, extracting muskrats from traps, re-setting traps that had been tripped, and adjusting some of the sets. With a towsack over one shoulder, containing the 'rats he had caught thus far, he neared the location where about two dozen head of cattle had been grazing, but suddenly had stopped their munching to watch this two-legged intruder on their range. Manson moved to within a hundred feet of the animals before halting and dropping the sack into the grass. After his customary moment of silence, he flailed his arms in the air and hollered at the bovine onlookers while taking another few steps in their direction. The expected stampede was sudden as the cattle whirled about amid a spattering of mud and water and, with tails lifted, headed for distant parts where perhaps no such monster would be interrupting their peaceful pursuit of nutrition.

One animal, however, stood its ground and appeared not so frightened by the trapper's antics. A large brown bull stiffly stood in defiance. The man stopped again and took a closer survey of the animal that held him in his sights. "That bull looked like he was eight feet tall and twelve feet long, but I know he couldn't have been," Manson would later recall. Maybe one more determined bluff would convince the bull that he had better turn and join the rest of the herd. The man repeated his fearsome moves, but the bull answered only with a snort and a pitching of his head. Manson knew he was now in big trouble.

Without even considering the distance back to his boat, Manson knew that an attempted retreat to the bayou was not an option. Besides, any such rapid move on his part would only embolden the animal to charge. The trapper recalled having stepped across a large, partially-rotten log lying on the ground a short distance before initiating his cow-scaring routine. The log, some twelve to fifteen inches in diameter, was the only thing in the grassy clearing besides his adversary and him. Slowly stepping backward, Manson chanced a fleeting glance back over his shoulder to make certain he was backing toward the log. Slowly and deliberately measuring his steps, he then kept his gaze intently on the bull. The animal would take three or four steps toward him at a time, then stop to return the stare as if constantly sizing up the man before him. Manson passed beside his sack which he had left on the ground, indicating to him that he was within a few feet of the log. Finally seeing the log in his lower peripheral vision, he slowly stepped backward across the horizontal barricade, being careful not to catch his boot on the top of it. Still in slow motion, he lay face down behind the log, parallel with its length, and couched himself snugly against its rough, decaying bark. In this position, he was able to raise only his head to peer over the log at the bull.

The large animal had continued his forward movement, broken by the intermittent halts, and now approached Manson's towsack in the grass. Lowering his head to sniff the unfamiliar object, he must have been somewhat offended by the smell of the muskrats inside as he snorted and quickly stuck his nose into the air, violently shaking his head. "Oh boy, he's really mad now," Manson thought as he kept his eyes on the bull from his prone position. The bull, not more than fifteen feet from the log, did not advance nearer Manson's location. Again smelling the sack, he looked to his right and left, apparently seeking the man. Then, the first positive sign from the animal appeared as he bit off a mouthful of grass and stood chewing it. After what seemed like hours, but actually consuming only two or three minutes, the bull apparently felt the human intruder had simply sunk into the marsh mud and contented himself to resume his grazing. He finally turned and slowly began bogging his way back in the direction of his bovine harem that had earlier fled so unceremoniously at Manson's aggressive motion.

After the bull had retreated to a safe distance from him, Manson arose from his position behind the log, retrieved his sack of 'rats, and made his way back toward his skiff on Rabbit Bayou. He still had more traps to run, but he would go to the other end of his trapline farther up the bayou to check the others. He would never again allow himself to be drawn so near to a herd of the wild marsh cattle without first making certain he had a means of escape should conditions take a turn for the worst.

Recounting his close call at Rabbit Bayou years later, Manson would declare with certainty: "I know that God put that log in the marsh for me. There was no way I could 'a got away from that bull without it."

· CHAPTER V ·

THE 1940's

The new decade arrived with yet another note of sadness for the Clark family as the elder William Clark died in February, 1940. Manson and Bill were trapping the Lawrence Marsh, south of Cotton Lake, at the time and were camped on the hillside at the western edge of the marsh near Alligator Bayou (at the site where is today located the Chambers County solid waste disposal area for Beach City). Word was brought to them of their father's death by Owen Maley.

By this time, economic recovery appeared to be well on the way throughout the country. The Great Depression era was being declared as a thing of the past. With the recovery came the strengthening of the market for wild furs and skins. The demand for furs increased, but area trappers soon found that the supply of furbearers in the Cove marshes was again at a low ebb. There simply were not enough animals in the Cove marshes to merit the full attention of the trappers.

Manson had already been looking for new trapping grounds. He and Bill were told of a large marsh area on the east side of Trinity Bay where the muskrats were making a strong comeback after a decade of relatively low population. They were told that the 'rats had never been trapped in the region nor had the alligators been hunted to any great degree. The area was the great expanse of marshland located south of Double Bayou, north of East Bay, and generally east of Smith Point. The marshes were part of the extensive rangeland of several large ranches of the region.

The trappers soon acquired trapping and hunting leases on the ranch marshlands of Elwood Wilborn and G. R. Canada. The deal agreed upon between the trappers and the ranchers was that the landowners would receive twenty-five percent of the gross income of the trappers which was derived from the ranchland marshes. No formal contracts were written; it was still the age in which the handshakes of honorable men meant more than their signatures on a piece of paper.

Inspecting the marshes, Manson and Bill found a veritable paradise for their line of work. Muskrat beds dotted the approximately three thousand acres under their lease and alligator dens were scattered throughout the marshes. The ranchers had built "cow roads" through the marshes. These were dirt roads built by draglines from the edge of the prairies and extending deep into the heart of the lowlands which afforded access for the cattle to the fertile grasslands of the marshes. The roads were some four to five feet in height, built from dirt and mud taken from the ground beside the roadbeds, creating canals or ditches parallel to the roads themselves.

It was at the very end of the main cow road into the marshes that Manson and Bill constructed a camphouse. The cabin was some fifteen by twenty feet in size and contained beds, butane cook stove, a table and other items deemed necessary for everyday living. The trappers knew that during the wet seasons they would be forced to stay at the camp for long periods of time due to the impassable condition of the mud roads. This, too, was during the days prior to the spanning of the Trinity River by any bridges in Chambers County and, since the earlier ferries across the rivers were no longer in operation, it was necessary to travel northward to Liberty, some twenty-five miles distant from Cove, to cross the river by automobile enroute to the camp. Therefore, the men usually made a week long excursion at a time, coming home to Cove only on Saturday afternoons, spending the night at home and attending Church the following morning, then returning Sunday afternoon to the camp.

The campsite was a virtual paradise for marshmen and lovers of nature. Located some three miles from the nearest public road, that being the lightly-traveled Double Bayou to Smith Point road, both days and nights offered a degree of solitude not often found elsewhere. Only the sounds of the wild could be detected, such as the mating call of the alligator, the sound of geese flying overhead, the playful quacking of ducks feeding on a nearby pond, and the thousands of field larks and jackdaw birds with which the marsh teemed. Occasionally one of the ranchers would visit the camp, or a couple of cowboys on horseback, out checking the cattle, would come by for a cup of coffee. If the trappers were in the marsh running their traplines, the visitors knew they were welcome to enter the cabin and heat a pot of coffee for themselves.

During the overlap period of the latter part of duck hunting season and the early days of the muskrat trapping season, Manson was torn between his two responsibilities of keeping his duck hunting guide service in operation on Cotton Lake at Cove and trapping the 'rats on the east side of the bay. It was obvious that he could not care for both at the same time. During this period he hired Gene Dutton, another lifelong Cove resident, to take care of the hunters at home during his absence. Himself reared in a family of trappers and hunters, Gene was a good choice for the work as his knowledge of nautical life and hunting techniques provided assurance that the Cotton Lake operations would continue without a hitch. A man of a pleasant and jovial nature, Dutton began referring to the city-slicker hunters as "clients."

With permission from Messrs. Wilborn and Canada, Manson and Bill began allowing a few of their relatives and friends to join them in hunting and trapping trips to their newfound retreat. Their younger brother, Vane, did a bit of trapping as did Manson's brother-in-law, Harley Maley. Occasional trips to the camp were also made by Arnold and Damon McKay, Charles Joseph, Jr., and others, all lifelong Cove residents and close friends or relatives of the Clarks.

This region contained an odd phenomenon of a terrain feature just east of the camp site. This was an area known as the Willow Marsh and was located on the Canada Ranch. About a half mile from the camphouse was a small lake which, as the trappers noticed soon after they moved into the region, literally changed shape overnight with each change in the direction of the wind. Closer investigation of the strange occurrence revealed that the land area surrounding the lake consisted only of surface soil, some eight to twelve inches thick, and the "ground" actually floated on the water. When the wind changed direction, the "floating turf" broke loose from one side of the lake and was blown across the body of water to make contact with the far side.

The trappers soon discovered it was impossible to walk very near the lake as the bottomless, muddy turf would not support the weight of a man. Slipping through the surface into the lake waters below could prove quite dangerous if the victim went completely beneath the turf and had to attempt to find a break in the sod through which to again emerge. For some distance into the marsh surrounding the floating turf area, the ground remained very unsettled and literally quivered beneath the footsteps of the trappers. The turf was covered with vegetation not unlike that which grew throughout the region and its instability could not be detected visually. G. R. Canada himself, owner of the ranchland, had been told of the floating turf by several of his ranch hands, but had never believed the stories to be entirely credible. Now, his trappers brought similar tales to him. One day while riding into the marshes himself to check on his cattle, Canada approached the lake. Suddenly, the ground gave way beneath his horse's hooves, man and beast alike disappearing below the surface. The man and his horse fought their way out of the perilous situation and back onto more stable ground. Canada remounted and rode away from the area, now convinced of the existence of the floating turf on his property.

The heavy population of alligators in the Willow Marsh country was borne out one night as Manson was hunting along a ditch in the marsh. It became his most successful single hunt in all his years of seeking the reptiles. Forty-two 'gators fell prey to his rifle that night. He later recalled that he could have taken even more alligators had he stayed on the waterway longer, but could not have loaded another 'gator into his skiff without sinking the craft.

Several lakes were within the massive expanse of marshland between the camp site and East Bay. One of them was known as Stephenson Lake and was reported to be teeming with buffalo fish. In 1941, Manson and Bill took a 1,350-foot long seine to the lake and within a few days caught more than eight thousand pounds of buffalo in its shallow waters. In November 1942, Manson's family grew again as Myra gave birth to a son whom they named Kendon Lee. With yet another mouth to feed in the family, there could be no easing of the challenge to work the marshes and waters for a livelihood.

■   ■   ■   ■   ■   ■   ■

During the summer months of the 1940's, when he was not hunting alligators in the marshes on the east side of the county, Manson devoted more time to his shrimping activities on Trinity Bay. His eldest daughter, Gloria, now in her early teenage years, often accompanied Manson on such trips. Not only did he commend his daughter as being a good deckhand in helping to cull the shrimp and fish after the net was hauled in, but he had the idea that she brought him good luck when she went along.

One day she and Elton "Toad" Hill, son of Ben Hill and grandson to Eli, went with Manson to the bay. The trawl was lowered overboard and the familiar "dragging" pattern was begun. Within minutes the boat began to slow in speed and the engine seemed unable to pull the net. Thinking he might have snagged a large log on the bay bottom, Manson stopped the boat and attempted to pull the trawl aboard. To his surprise, he found the net loaded with shrimp and fish, obviously having dragged through a large school of shrimp. The trawl was so heavy with the little creatures that they were unable to lift it into the boat. He reasoned that his daughter had really brought him good fortune that day, but it would do little good if they were not able to load the shrimp. Scanning the open bay, Manson detected a boat several hundred yards from his position and managed to attract the attention of its occupant. The boat coming toward them, they soon recognized the man as Jesse Fayle, himself out for a day on the water. Jesse's boat was rigged with a small boompole with which they were able to load the heavy cargo into Manson's boat. After an exchange of thanks with Jesse, Manson headed the boat for home as Gloria and Elton began culling through the contents of the net.

■　■　■　■　■　■　■

Electricity came to Cove in 1946, and Manson had made up his mind to take advantage of this marvelous new luxury by purchasing a freezer. The contraption was one of the chest type, then known as a "deep freeze." With this equipment, he could keep shrimp, fish, ducks or rabbits for an indefinite period of time without fear of their spoiling before usage.

Soon after his acquisition of the freezer, Manson came in from the bay with a successful haul of shrimp. The brand new freezer had never been used and Manson plugged its cord into an electrical outlet to allow it to begin cooling. As the freezer hummed in its generation of cold air inside, Manson summarily beheaded the shrimp, washed the edible bodies, and then dumped the entire lot into the freezer from No. 3 tubs. He had not been informed that the shrimp should be placed in bags or other containers to separate them from direct contact with the floor and walls of the cold box. He assumed that each shrimp would simply freeze individually.

When the day came for the shrimper to haul his catch to market, he went to the freezer to remove the shrimp. What he found taught him a lesson he would never forget. The shrimp were all frozen together in one huge block, the block equally frozen solidly to the freezing compartment itself. The shrimp would not budge from their positions. Manson had already learned how rapidly shrimp tend to spoil if left unchilled, so disconnecting the freezer to allow them to thaw out was discounted. With no alternate remedy at hand, Manson turned to his hatchet and began hacking away at the frozen mass of shrimp. It was quite some time before the last of the seafood was finally removed from the freezer, an untold number of the little bodies having been unceremoniously chopped in half during the process. From that day forward, shrimp and all other bare-bodied creatures were placed in containers of some sort before being committed to the depths of the freezing compartment.

In July 1947, Manson made what became probably the most publicized hunt of his career as a marshman. Chester Rogers, outdoor reporter for *The Houston Chronicle*, went along with Manson on an alligator hunt in the Trinity River bottomlands with the hope of obtaining a story about the marshman and his

65

trade. Alligators were quite a novelty to most of Chester's readers in the big city of Houston and the thought of anyone actually seeking out the ferocious-looking reptiles made some of them wonder just how far our society had advanced from the pioneer period.

During several previous hunts in this area, Manson had seen the drag of a large alligator through breaks in the seacane and in shallow marsh sloughs between Trinity and Lost Rivers. An odd feature about this alligator's trail was that only three footprints were visible in the mud where the drag was found. On this expedition, Manson had determined he would track the large 'gator to his den if at all possible.

Locating the trail in the dense seacane and twill grass, Manson told Chester they were going to follow the drag as long as they could "read" the sign in the mud. Through the boggy terrain they progressed with Manson in the lead, breaking a trail through the cane while keeping a close watch for unwelcome cottonmouths. Finally, there was the object of their search; a small pond of some fifteen by thirty feet in size completely surrounded by the thick, overgrown vegetation. On one side of the pond stood an aging growth of willow trees, wearily drooping its limbs out over the water. Amid the roots was the mouth of the tunnel where the marsh denizen lay.

As Manson made his way around the edge of the pit to a position directly above the tunnel, Chester snapped some photographs of the eerie scene with his camera. Positioned in the seacane behind the watery den, Manson began driving the iron rod into the soft earth and soon located the hollow tunnel beneath the marsh ground. Then, he felt the hard, scaly back of the 'gator with the rod and began the process of "tickling" the reptile. Suddenly, the water on the surface of the pond began to rise, or "swell" as it is often termed by the marshmen, as the creature inside the tunnel began crawling toward the open pit. Noting the movement of the surface water, Manson took up his rifle and silently awaited the appearance of the alligator. Chester, stationed on the far side of the pond, remained motionless with his camera ready. Then, a pair of eyes emerged from the water near the mouth of the tunnel, practically invisible to the untrained human eye. As Manson took careful aim, Chester quietly snapped another photograph. Suddenly, the sharp crack of the rifle abruptly broke the surface of the water and the pair of eyes disappeared. It was all over.

Chester helped Manson pull the heavy creature out of the pond. Slowly the great reptile was dragged onto the muddy ground – all thirteen feet and six inches of him. Despite his length, the 'gator was quite slim in stature, but still tipped the scales at 812 pounds. Had he been in full physical condition, the creature would doubtless have rounded out a complete one thousand pounds. Neither the length nor the weight of this specimen was its most notable feature, however. The two men noticed that the right front foot of the alligator was missing, thereby accounting for the three-tracked trail Manson had seen in the marshes on several occasions previously. The nub of the leg was completely healed and covered with thick hide. Manson reasoned that the foot had probably been lost many years earlier in a fight with another, larger alligator and had merely been bitten off. Before leaving the marsh with the heavy hide, Manson and Chester had already dubbed the reptile with the name "Old Nub Foot." The word "Old" in the creature's name was quite fitting, as things soon developed. Biologists who studied the information relating to the alligator estimated his age to be some one thousand years. "Old Nub Foot" truly fit the image which had often been applied to members of his species, that of being a hold over from the Prehistoric Age.

Chester Rogers wrote a special feature story for the *Chronicle*, replete with photographs of the day's hunt. Not only did "Old Nub Foot" receive local fame from the newspaper article, but a color photograph of Manson skinning the reptile in the marsh was sold to a company for publication on picture postcards. In subsequent years, the postcards were reportedly seen on card racks in stores throughout Texas, as well as in Louisiana and Arkansas. Manson was to have received twenty-five percent of the sales from the cards, although decades later had never collected the first penny from the proceeds.

■　■　■　■　■　■　■

At home in Cove, Manson thought about a project he had considered for several years. For some thirty-five years he had been guiding duck hunters on Cotton Lake during the fall and winter months. Throughout that period, he and his hunters had trod a narrow boardwalk across the marsh from the hillside to the lakeshore where he kept the hunting boats secured. Now, in 1947, he obtained permission from his mother-in-law, Mrs. Genevra Maley, to have a channel dug across the marsh in order that he might keep his boats at a landing at the base of the hillside. Manson hired Bob Harmon and his dragline for the project and the job was completed before the opening of the duck season in November.

■　■　■　■　■　■　■

When Manson's daughters, Gloria and Freda, came of the age to be allowed to begin dating boyfriends during the decade of the 1940's, Freda saw what she considered as a real hindrance to her social activities in the form of her daddy's fur trapping business. Manson had not yet built a "drying shack" separate from the family home in which to dry the raw muskrat skins he brought in from the marsh during the winter months. During periods of damp weather, when the skins could not be left outdoors for the curing process, they were brought inside the home for drying. Such was a job which could not be delayed, especially during wet spells, lest the pelts begin to deteriorate in value.

Freda always hoped for beautiful weather for outside fur drying when she had a young male escort coming to take her out. She told Manson that the hides, propped on various items in the living room, was a source of great embarrassment to her when her prospective suitors came to their home. Nevertheless, the fur drying had to proceed.

When the boyfriend did arrive and entered the home, the first thing he would notice, naturally, was the array of fur in the living room. More often than not, the young man would take a seat and eagerly begin asking Manson about his hunting and trapping experiences and appeared none too hurried about leaving the home for the scheduled date. This caused Manson to tease his daughter about her dislike of the home-drying of the furs, inferring that what she really did not like about the practice was that the furs were in "competition" with her for the attention of the young men who came to escort her. Later, Manson pulled from the water an old houseboat he had owned for years, set it up on his property away from the family home, and converted it into a drying house for the furs.

■　■　■　■　■　■　■

Rabbit hunting continued to be a major supplementary source of work during the winter months. One night Manson, Bill, and Lawrence Schaeffer, another of their Cove neighbors, made a hunt in the vicinity of Jack's Pass, near the mouth of the Trinity River and not far from Anahuac. At the mouth of the Pass was a large cove off Trinity Bay known as Jack's Pocket, a shallow, silt-filled mud cove which often went dry during windy wintertime northers. As usual, the three decided to separate from each other and take individual routes. Manson left the boat on the east side of Garden Bayou, a dead end stream which cut northward through the marshes from Jack's Pocket. Bill and Lawrence would walk near the bayshore and into open marsh areas where their headlights might catch the red glow of a rabbit's eye.

Walking a short distance from the bank of Garden Bayou, Manson soon found himself in a large growth of thigh-high black weeds, which often provided good protection and cover for rabbits. Stepping upon an old half-rotten log lying at the edge of the growth of weeds, he stood his six-foot frame on the elevated position and scanned the darkness of the weeds for the eye of a swamp rabbit. There was one. Shouldering his weapon, he squeezed the trigger and the rabbit fell, exposing its white belly in the glare of the headlight. Without moving, lest his footsteps scare away another of the rodents hiding in the weeds, he quietly slipped another shell into the gun and again slowly scanned the weeds with his light. There's another one. And the same process was repeated. Standing on the log without moving from his position, Manson shot twenty-five shells within a few minutes. Lawrence and Bill, walking the marsh a short distance from him, could not help but wonder what he was doing in firing so many shots. Manson heard Lawrence call across the marsh to Bill, "Do you reckon Manson's killing a rabbit with every shot?"

Finally, Manson poured the light over the weed growth one final time until he was satisfied there were no more rabbits there. For the first time since taking his position on the log, he stepped to the ground, combed the dark weeds, and found all twenty-five of his swamp rabbits.

He had one more box of twenty-five shells in his possession that night with which he rounded out a total of fifty rabbits. Added to those killed by Bill and Lawrence, the three hunters had more than a hundred swamp rabbits to haul to market the following day.

Manson's astounding kill of half his rabbits while standing still on the log served to convince him even more of the importance of employing as little movement as possible when hunting the furry rodents. The gunshots did not appear to frighten the rabbits away, but rather caused them to look up from their feeding so that the glow of their eyes could be detected in his headlight beam. Had he stepped off the log to retrieve the first rabbit he had shot, his footsteps would likely have spooked the remainder away from the growth of weeds and out of his sight.

■ ■ ■ ■ ■ ■ ■

The decade of the 1940's was rife with hurricanes and tropical storms along the Texas coast. The region was struck in 1941, and in 1943 a storm which was to have gone inland down the coast near Corpus Christi took a northeastward turn and followed the coastline to the Galveston Bay area before making landfall. Yet another storm had slammed into the area in 1945. The decade would similarly come to an end in an equally destructive manner.

One day during the late summer of 1949, the wind began to noticeably increase from the northeast which, during this time of the year, was rare except in the northern extremities of the circular motion of a hurricane. Throughout the day the wind intensified and rain began to fall. Overhead, the clouds boiled and wrestled with each other as if vying for position in the heavens.

Realizing the potential for a storm that night, Manson, his wife, and son loaded into the family car that afternoon and drove to Goose Creek, over in Harris County, to secure a new battery for the radio, as well as other provisions which might be needed during the days following a storm. Returning in the direction of Cove, darkness settled about them earlier than usual due to the heavy cloud cover. Just east of Cedar Bayou, they stopped at a KTRH radio transmitter station where Manson went inside to ask the men what was happening in the way of weather. Sure enough, the radio workers related to him, a storm was indeed moving into the area from the Gulf of Mexico, although they were not certain as yet as to its potential.

Hurrying home, Manson decided he had to take his hunting boats to Cotton Bayou. If left on the open marshy area on the north side of Cotton Lake, they would be dashed to pieces by the wind and waves when the gale's wind direction finally "went around" and came from a southerly direction, bringing the full thrust of the storm against them. Cotton Bayou was heavily wooded on either side and would afford a greater amount of protection from the winds and seas.

Proceeding to his recently-dug landing, Manson tied the hunting skiffs in a line, one behind the other, with the mooring ropes, and then tied the lead boat to his own motorized craft. Out the mouth of the slip into to the darkness of the windswept lake he moved slowly, his marine caravan strung out behind him like a loose-jointed serpent. Turning southwestward toward Cotton Bayou, he found that the northeast wind had increased to a point as to make it necessary for him to travel as near the north shore of the lake as possible where the bluff hillside and woods afforded some protection from the wind. Moving across the lake's northwest corner known as Ernest Cove, so termed because of the proximity of the Ernest Winfree homesite atop the hillside, Manson finally entered the narrow mouth of Cotton Bayou and led his boats upstream into the thickness of the woods.

Manson tied the boats to trees along the north bank of the bayou, being certain to allow enough rope for the boats to rise as the tide began to roll in. As he was completing this task, the wind began to change direction, coming from the south. The center of the storm was obviously moving inland somewhere just west of Cove and Manson knew the worst of the storm was yet to come. The back side of the hurricane with its powerful southerly winds would bring the waters of the Gulf across the marshes to slam against the highland.

Manson hurriedly scaled the hillside to begin his walk back through the woods toward home. It was now "raining sideways" as the terrific south wind drove the precipitation horizontally across the hillside. But, the rain was not his greatest worry. The extremely thick cloud cover above the storm created the blackest night Manson ever remembered. He held his hand before his face, but found it to be invisible to his sight. He had no flashlight with which to guide his footsteps in the total darkness. His only hope of reaching home was to attempt to walk along the top of the hillside at the point where the highland breaks downward to fall to the lakeshore and marshes. If he began to veer too far off course, he should be able to feel the descent down the hillside. It would take all his knowledge of the terrain, as well as a guiding hand from his merciful Creator, to find his way back home this night.

As he slowly felt his way northeastward, the wind continued to increase in velocity and a new sound came to his ears. Trees were beginning to give way before the mighty winds, the cracking of their limbs and crashing of their trunks to the ground causing him to wonder when one might fall across him, pinning him to the soggy ground. At intervals, he found it necessary to drop to his hands and knees to crawl along beneath the underbrush in order to maintain his course along the break of the hillside, a route which he knew he must maintain if he were to reach home tonight.

What if he crawled within reach of a cottonmouth? The poisonous snakes were doubtless being flushed out of the marshes and onto the highland by the rapidly rising tides. In such a state of annoyance, the serpents were usually angry and ready to strike anything that moved. He attempted to put that thought from his mind as there was little he could do to control that element anyway.

Ambling along the hillside in the deafening wind, Manson reached and crossed Black Gully, a usually dry washout which extended a short distance into the Winfree woods from the marshes. This landmark indicated to him that he was at least halfway to his destination. After what seemed an eternity, he finally reached a barbed wire fence stretched across his path and extending down the hill to the marsh. This had to be the property line between the Winfree and Maley lands, which meant that Manson's boat landing was not more than a hundred yards ahead. Squeezing between the strands of barbed wire, he walked the final distance to the shelter of his pickup truck where he had some difficulty in opening the door of the vehicle against the powerful wind. Inside, he slowly drove the half mile back home, fatigued almost to his limit, but ever so thankful to be back among his family.

With the morning light, the storm had spent its fury and its winds of more than one hundred miles per hour during the night had lessened to a gusty breeze. Manson climbed back into his truck and headed for his boat landing. The sight which greeted him almost turned his stomach. Great masses of seacane, logs and other debris had been swept from the marshes and hurled inland against the hillside by the wind and waves of the storm. Halted by the incline of the hillside from further intrusion, the two-to-three-foot-thick mass of tangled wreckage floated on the surface of the water of the landing and slip. The facility he had had built for his business was completely useless in its present state. Only one recourse was open to him if he ever intended to use the landing again; the debris had to be cleared from the water and it had to be done before the logs and other objects had time to become water-logged and sink to the bottom of the landing. Neighbors told Manson that such was an impossible task, that he would be better off to simply abandon the landing. However, the marshman did not see it that way. He at least had to make an attempt.

For thirty days, Manson worked at the landing. Chopping the tangled masses of drift into smaller mats or rafts with a hatchet, he positioned the bow of his motorboat atop the portions of wreckage and slowly pushed them out the mouth of the slip and onto the waters of Cotton Lake where they were turned loose and allowed to drift ashore elsewhere. With wire stretchers and "comealongs" he pulled huge logs and trees out of the landing and onto its banks. A common garden rake was used to drag lighter mats of seacane and debris from the water. After a full month, he was able to declare the task completed, the water in the slip, from the hillside to the lake, again open for his boat traffic.

■ ■ ■ ■ ■ ■ ■

On an alligator hunt in the marsh during the summer of 1949, he made a kill which, turned into a lifelong alligator "baby sitting" task for him. As a rule, Manson would not kill a female alligator if he found that she had a nest of eggs nearby. However, on this day he had already killed a young "she 'gator" before he located her nest in the seacane near the den. Realizing that the unguarded nest would become a target for marsh predators and the eggs therein would probably become a meal for a hungry coon if left in the nest, Manson determined to take the eggs home with him to see if any of them might hatch under different conditions. Digging into the mound of compressed mud and seacane, he located twenty-eight eggs. Gently placing them in a towsack without cracking any of the shells, he brought them out of the marsh and took them home.

Manson fashioned a man-made "nest" in the southwest section of the family yard at home, a few feet from his vehicle garage and beneath the boughs of a patch of cane he had planted several years earlier. Placing the eggs in the makeshift nest, he stood and viewed his creation. Perhaps his nest was not of the same dimensions as one which would be found in the marsh, and some old female 'gator would probably find reasons to criticize his handiwork, but it looked like a masterpiece of marsh construction to him.

Applying a small amount of water to the surface of the nest about every other day and allowing the sun to bake its surface on a daily basis, it began to take on more the appearance of the real thing as days passed. The nest began to look so real, in fact, that Manson decided he had better make arrangements to care for his reptile progeny in the event any of the eggs did hatch. He dug a small hole near the nest and filled it with water. A long sheet of tin was bent about a couple of posts and fastened at each end to the outside wall of the garage, forming a pen some four feet in diameter. Now, he was ready in the event anything happened.

On a day in early September, things did begin to happen. The eggs inside the nest began to crack and out came the little alligators. Manson was thrilled as he watched his adopted offspring emerge from the nest one by one and instinctively dart directly for the water hole he had prepared. A few of the little fellows were obviously having a difficult time trying to crack their eggshells, so with the care of a concerned parent, Manson took these few eggs into his home and cracked the eggs himself, then placed them in a container on the kitchen cabinet while the reptiles completed their emergence from the shells. Myra did not think too highly of her kitchen cabinet top being used as a delivery table for infant alligators, but managed to keep her thoughts to herself, not wanting to be the source of dampening the happy occasion. As the little 'gators emerged from their shells, Manson carried the six-to-seven-inch-long reptiles to the pen by the garage where they joined their sisters in the water hole. 'Twas a joyous day at the Clark home as all twenty-eight of the eggs hatched out within a period of a few hours.

The newly-hatched alligators formed what would later prove to be a female litter. Shortly after the egg-hatching event, Manson would happen upon another 'gator hole in the marsh where the heads of several slightly larger young alligators appeared curious at his approach. Kneeling beside the edge of the pit, he managed to catch two of the little reptiles whose curiosity brought them within his reach. Judging from their length of about twelve or so inches, it was clear to him that they were from a litter hatched by their mother the previous year. Placing them in a towsack, he brought them home where they were added to his growing "herd." It would later become obvious that these two new additions were bull 'gators.

Through the coming years, Manson would observe the alligators closely and learn much more about the creatures than he had already learned from his many years in the marshes. He would learn that they were a very gluttonous lot during their early years, eating just about everything offered to them. Once they reached a length of some five to six feet, however, their appetites would be reduced dramatically and the larger they grew, the less they ate. He brought in scrap fish from his shrimping excursions during the summer to feed the hungry mouths. The 'gators were no trouble at all during the months of late fall and winter as they ate nothing whatsoever between the months of October and March, which included their hibernation period.

Years later, when the alligators attained breeding age. the females fought each other like demons for the attentions of the larger bull 'gators. This ritual would continue each spring. Manson found, as he had long suspected, that the wildlife books written about alligators were rife with mistakes. One of the most obvious errors in the literary works was the claim that only the bull alligators practiced the roaring mating call as he sought out his mate for the spring. Too many times Manson observed his alligators in the pen, males and females alike, with their heads raised from the pit, giving their mating call (known to 'gator hunters as "bellering") to all who would listen.

When the alligators had reached a length of some two feet, their natural instinct of tunneling into the ground brought about a problem. In their original home pen, they had dug their tunnel beneath the garage in which the family car was kept. Since they were not able to dig as deeply beneath the surface of the hard, highland ground as their cousins in the soft, muddy earth of the marshes, only a few inches of surface soil separated the tunnel from the dirt floor of the garage. The inevitable finally happened one day when one of the wheels of the car, parked inside the enclosure, caved in through the tunnel. Finding a ready exit through the collapsed tunnel, alligators escaped and scattered in all directions. Some were even found beneath the wood frame family home while others made their getaway via a nearby gully. Most were recovered, however, and the tunnel was repaired. A larger pen, some forty by fifty feet in size, was later built to house the reptiles – this time a safe distance away from any garage or building.

Some thirty years later, only two of the homegrown alligators would remain with the Clark family, the remainder having escaped through the years, with the exception of a couple of unfortunate females who had been killed during the ferocious springtime battles with their sisters. At this writing (1983), an eleven-foot-long bull alligator and a female some eight and one-half feet in length remain as the family pets, if indeed the word "pet" can be applied in such cases.

• CHAPTER VI •

THE 1950's

During the late 1940's, Manson had been doing more and more shrimping on Trinity Bay. He had used an inboard boat of some twenty feet in length which had been bought from a man named Joe Dubose, the craft named the "Mary Lou" after the wife of the original owner.

Shrimping was rapidly becoming more of a way of life during the summer months for those men who chose to make their livelihood from the fruits of nature. Manson decided that if this line of work was going to consume such a great part of his summer work time, he should have a boat capable of standing up to the rough waters of the bay and carrying everything he needed for successful excursions on the open water. In 1949, he had contracted with his old friend, Saylus Elliott, who lived near the mouth of Cedar Bayou on lower West Bay, to construct for him a commercial shrimping vessel with a length of thirty-five feet. Now, in 1950, the craft was ready for use, having been built in Saylus' back yard near the bank of Cedar Bayou. The boat was christened the "Freda," named after Manson's youngest daughter.

She was a beauty, her glistening white hull rising some four feet above the waterline along her work decks and the high bow rising to some six feet, designed to split the waves of Trinity Bay. She had a hold beneath her deck with a capacity to haul hundreds of pounds of shrimp and ice. Her cabin would sleep from two to four deck hands comfortably and the wheelhouse behind the cabin was so situated as to make her captain feel he was the master of her destiny. Towering above the cabin rose the mast, twenty feet high above the deck, to which was attached a large boompole for the purpose of dragging in the shrimp trawl and depositing its contents on the deck. The vessel was propelled by a six-cylinder Gray engine.

The work completed and the craft considered seaworthy by both her owner and builder, the "Freda" was launched into the waters of Cedar Bayou. The engine was started and allowed to idle in neutral for several minutes while final investigations were made for any errors. Within minutes, the smell of gasoline fumes was detected in the cabin and engine room. Quickly shutting off the engine, Manson soon located the problem. A nail had been driven through the timbers and protruded far enough to puncture a fuel line near the engine. Calling Saylus to inspect the imperfection, the problem was soon remedied by the veteran seaman, and the "Freda" was officially pronounced seaworthy. Built and completely rigged at a cost of some $1,800, she was now ready for the open water.

Running at slow speed out the mouth of Cedar Bayou, Manson entered Trinity Bay for the vessel's maiden voyage to her home port at Cove. She was brought into Old River and put into dock at the old Pure Oil Company landing. Arriving at the wharf there, Manson found that it had not taken long for word to get around in Cove that the new boat was coming. He was surprised to see quite a crowd of his relatives and neighbors gathered at the landing, some taking snapshots as the vessel approached. He obliged some of the well-wishers with a brief cruise up the river a short distance and back to the landing. In later years, the "Freda" was docked at Arnold F. McKay's boat landing at Hugo Point in Cove. Still later, Manson had an extension dug into his own boat landing on Cotton Lake to accommodate the vessel.

While he made some considerable catches with the boat, Manson later came to realize that there was not much more money to be made with the larger boat than with smaller ones he had used before. One always had to take into consideration the additional expenses of running and maintaining a larger boat as well as the added difficulty in caring for its life. Manson had a large set of quays built at his boat landing for the purpose of hauling the boat out on land each year. It was then that all the barnacles had to be removed from her hull and a fresh coat of copper paint applied around her bottom.

Some of the better days of shrimping with the "Freda" produced upwards of seven hundred pounds of saleable shrimp, but such days were few and far between. When he returned home in the afternoons with his catch, the work had only begun. Those were the days of a great supply of shrimp in the bay waters which thereby kept the demand at a lesser point. The heads had to be removed from the shrimp before they could be sold – not because of game laws, but because of consumer preference. Manson hired several local Cove residents who regularly worked in the shrimphouse for him, beheading the shrimp until the late night hours.

Probably the most income Manson ever realized from the use of the "Freda" was not from shrimping at all, but rather in conveying the crewmen of an oil drilling rig to and from their work site on Mustang Island, south of Cotton Lake, where drilling operations were being conducted. The company contracted with Manson to use his shrimpboat in the changing of shifts every eight hours. He also had to remain on a standby status to convey company officials to the site at any hour of the day or night which they might require. The crewmen met Manson's boat at Mann Wilburn's landing, located just off Hugo Point. They were transported through Hugo Bayou, down a portion of Cross Bayou, and then to Mustang Island via a man-made ditch cut across the marshes of the "Potlikker Hunting Club" between Cotton Lake and Wet Marsh Pond.

■ ■ ■ ■ ■ ■ ■

The 1950's brought telephone service to Cove. The wires were strung down Gou Hole Road as far as its intersection with the private road which continued southward to Manson Clark's boat landing. Manson's home was situated at the intersection and consequently was the site of the southernmost telephone on the line. Although the system began in Cove with eight-to-ten phone partylines, it nevertheless better enabled Manson's duck hunters to call days in advance of their proposed hunting date to reserve a boat and blind (the telephone number was a simple "4626"). Manson had by now developed quite a business with his duck hunting guide service on Cotton Lake and hunters came from as far away as Dallas for a single day's hunt. He operated at least a dozen hunting skiffs and annually built some twenty duck blinds on the lake.

Some of his hunters had been customers for many years and the family looked forward to renewing acquaintances with them each fall and winter. One man who had been hunting with Manson since the 1930"s was Harry Meyer of Houston. He had become almost like one of the family and Gloria, Freda and Kendon had even taken to referring to him as "Uncle Harry." A native of Mississippi, Harry had been through a fortune earlier in his life and now operated a used car dealership in Houston. On weekends, he was allowed to stay overnight in the old houseboat Manson had converted into a fur drying house in the family yard, affording him the opportunity to hunt both Saturday and Sunday of each week without having to return to Houston for the night. During World War II, when items had to be purchased with an accompanying ration stamp, Harry aided the family in passing on to them such stamps as he did not use himself. He continued to hunt with Manson on Cotton Lake until becoming too feeble with age to continue his beloved activity.

Another of the regular hunters at the Clark hunting camp was a man who went by the name of Murray, also from Houston. This tall, lanky man hunted usually during the weekdays, his business keeping him in Houston during the weekends. He always hunted alone and was one of the most agreeable men to frequent Cotton Lake, never showing any preference as to which blind or boat he was allotted for his day's hunt. One of the most memorable features about Murray was that he always wore an old tattered, lightweight sport coat, gray in color, even on the coldest, most disagreeable days on the lake. He never wore gloves and only rarely a cap to insulate himself from the cold north winds. For years, the man was believed to be perfectly terrible in his lack of ability to hit ducks with his shotgun blasts. Even when the duck hunting was exceptionally good, Murray would rarely come in from his hunt with more than a couple of ducks to show for his effort, although he might have shot a dozen or more shells. One morning he came for a hunt and told Manson he did not have a gun. He had been renting a shotgun from a friend all these years, and the other man was in need of it himself this day. Asking Manson if he might have a shotgun he could rent, Manson offered his own gun to him free of charge for the morning hunt. Murray went to the blind that morning and found that he could not miss a shot! Every time he squeezed the trigger, a duck fell. He came in from the lake a couple hours later, excited over the fact that he had killed his legal bag limit for the day. Talking with Manson over a cup of coffee, the hunting guide explained to him that the gun he had been using through the years, and with which he had always had such bad luck, apparently did not "fit him." "A gun has to fit the hunter," explained Manson, "just like a shirt. A man has to be comfortable with a gun or he can't hit anything with it." Murray returned to Houston that day with his bag of ducks and immediately purchased for himself a Browning automatic shotgun exactly like Manson's firearm. From that day forward, Murray became a successful hunter on Cotton Lake.

The hunters would gather early in the mornings at the Clark home between 4:30 and 5:00 AM. They would be offered coffee, sitting around the living room, usually talking about past hunting trips, until the time came to leave for the blinds. Although Manson preferred that the hunters pay for their hunt prior to leaving the house, he was not one of the nature to ask for the money. This had resulted in several occasions when onetime hunters would come in from the lake early and leave without having paid for the services. Another man from Houston who had become a regular hunter on Cotton Lake noticed this after several hunts at Clark's place. He was Warren Taliaferro, a man who came to be known by the family as "The Irishman." Noting this laxity in the collecting of the hunting fees at the house in the mornings, Warren would wait until the house was full of hunters, all anxiously awaiting the time to leave for the lake. Then, he would come into the living room among the hunters, hand his fee to Manson, and announce, "It's about time to pay up so we can head for the lake." The other men would then eagerly come forward with their fees, ready to begin the day's hunt. Taliaferro would be one of Manson's most dependable hunters for as long as he guided duck hunters on Cotton Lake.

After the preliminaries were taken care of at the house, the hunters would drive the short distance to Manson's boat landing at the old Joe Maley place. There, the hunting boats were kept moored to wharves along the bank at the foot of the highland, each skiff equipped with approximately thirty duck decoys, a pair of oars, a mudpole (for navigating in shallow water) and a bailing bucket (for those frequent rainy days).

After the men had boarded their boats, usually two to three hunters per skiff, the boats were tied together one behind the other, much like the cars of a waterborne freight train, Manson's motor boat taking its position at the head of the column. It was at this point that any novice hunter who might need assistance in arranging his decoys at the blind, or someone who needed to return from the lake at a particular time was given the opportunity to speak up. Cranking the outboard engine, Manson proceeded out the boat slip and onto Cotton Lake, followed by the string of boats laden with hunters and their gear.

From one blind to another Manson towed the boats, the last skiff in the column being turned loose at each blind. The hunters often expressed amazement at how Manson could find all the blinds on the open lake in the predawn darkness, especially when the lake was shrouded in a cover of fog. Manson was the first to confess that locating the blinds in heavy fog was quite a chore. When he entered the lake from the boat slip on foggy mornings, his first act was to notice the direction of the ripples on the water and guide himself across the lake with the direction of the breeze as an indicator. If the cloud cover was not too thick overhead, he would note the position of the stars in the sky for use in the slow navigation about the lake. "I got lost many a time though," he would admit. "The main thing was to keep the hunters from knowing I was turned around. Some of those people would go crazy if they learned we were lost in the fog." With the many blinds he had on Cotton Lake, Manson was often amazed at how far he could move across the lake without happening across one of them. In the thickest fog, it was possible to pass within forty yards of a blind and never see it. It is on such occasions that fog plays many tricks on the human eye. There were times when he would spot the dim outline of a duck blind through the fog and turn his boat in that direction. Wide-eyed, attempting to keep the blind in sight until reaching its location, the blind would suddenly appear to actually be moving across the water like a motorboat and he seemed unable to navigate to catch up to it. On one occasion when Manson became "turned around" in heavy fog on the lake, with a string of hunting boats behind him, he suddenly saw what he interpreted as the Winfree woods looming up out of the fog directly ahead. He reasoned that he had become completely turned around in the fog and was heading back to the north side of the lake. The massive twenty-five-foot embankment of what he took to be the hillside loomed larger and larger with the trees along the crest of the hill. Suddenly, his outboard motor propeller dug into the mud and sand of the shallow water along the shore. Upon closer observation, he saw that he was almost aground on the south shore of the lake and what he had taken to be the hillside and trees was only the fifteen-inch-high bank of the marshes and the seacane along the shore. In such cases, Manson always believed that man simply was not meant to navigate a boat in foggy weather.

Each of the blinds on Cotton Lake had its own name for use in identification. Some were named for their location, such as: Bayou Blind, Mullet Slough, First Mullet Slough, Second Mullet Slough, Horse Island, Middle, West Middle, First Middle, Ernest Cove, Cotton Bayou Point, and Gougee Bayou Cove. Others wore the names of men who had hunted from the blinds frequently, or former owners of the blind sites: George Wilburn Blind (previous owner), Hadaway Blind (longtime hunter), Basil Blind (Basil Dutton), Mitchell Blind (Mitchell Rossi), Harley Blind (Harley Maley), Thurman Blind (Thurman Maley), Harry Blind (Harry Meyer), Leo Blind (Leo Morris), and Jamie Blind (James Hoffman). Two other blinds located on Cotton Lake during the 1950's were those of R. R. Harrington and Thomas J. Troutman, both Cove residents who lived on Cotton Bayou.

Manson could recall when the daily legal bag limit on ducks was fifty per day. In later years, it was lowered to twenty-five, then fifteen, then ten. During the 1950's, the daily limit stood at five ducks and several of the lifelong hunters of Cove did not consider this number to be worth the trouble of going to the marshes. Most of the wide variety of ducks to be found in the Central Flyway frequented Cotton Lake at intervals. The most numerous were bluebills (scaup), green wing teal, baldpates and pintails (sprigs), but hunters also brought in kills of mallards, gadwalls (bay ducks), canvasbacks, redheads, blue wing teal, and an occasional wood duck, ringneck duck, or cinnamon teal.

Early morning and late afternoon goose flights often provided additional "big game" shooting overhead. During the early morning hours, the geese left their marshland roosting areas to fly northward to the harvested rice fields on the highland for a day of feeding. Before dark, they could be seen lined up for miles across the sky in the familiar V-shaped formations, heading back southward to roost in the marshes for the night.

Generally, if nothing else was moving on the lake during any given day, a hunter could count on bringing in some amount of meat for the table in the form of the little black and white bluebill ducks, two forms of which are known officially to biologists as the greater and lesser scaup. The little ducks exhibited what appeared to be an overwhelming urge for constant companionship. At times when the lake was quite covered with hunters, a flock of some fifteen to twenty bluebills might begin their flight across the body of water, usually beginning at the east end of the lake near Mullet Slough, and stop at nearly every set of decoys they came to. The occupants of each blind would usually kill one, two or three of them, and the remainder would move on to the next blind site. Often not more than two or three of the original number of the flock would survive to reach the far end of the lake.

■   ■   ■   ■   ■   ■   ■

During the late 1940's, a new form of wildlife had been quietly introduced into the marshes which would soon change the complexion and lifestyle of the lowlands of Chambers County, and all of southeast Texas, as nothing had since the advent of the muskrats in 1915. Outdoor magazines carried advertisements promoting the sale of a species of a large, brown rodent known as the nutria. From the beginning, the name was used incorrectly as the actual name of the animal was the coypu (pronounced "ky-poo") and the word nutria was only correct in referring to the fur of the coypu. Due to the almost universal use of the word nutria in reference to the animal itself, we shall here employ that terminology.

The nutria was advertised as a deterrent to overgrowth of vegetation on marshland duck ponds and waterways. To be certain, the ads thusly stated were not misrepresentative of the animal. The live nutria, natives of South America, were sold for upwards of fifty dollars per pair from breeders across the country.

In the lower central Chambers County marshes near the area where Manson Clark and his associates had the Canada and Wilborn ranches under lease, Ralph Barrow, another extensive landowner and rancher, purchased several pairs of nutria for the purposes so stated above and turned them loose in his ranchland marshes. On the west side of the county in the Cove marshes, C. B. Delhomme of Houston, owner of a hunting club in the marshes between Cross Bayou and Cove Bayou, made a similar purchase for what was hoped would be a beneficial addition to his marshes.

One morning in 1950, while running his muskrat trapline in the Wilborn Ranch marshes, Manson came upon a trap which held one of these animals. The large ratlike rodent of some two feet in length immediately turned in the trap to face Manson and revealed a double pair of awesome orange-colored teeth. The animal emitted a plaintive, but defiant whine and sat back on its hindquarters as if ready for an attack. Manson was not exactly certain as to what the animal was, but recalled having attended a carnival in Goose Creek a decade ago in which one of these rodents was exhibited and billed as a "Giant South American Rat." Sizing up the little eight-inch-long billyclub he carried to kill muskrats in the traps, he had reservations about approaching this creature with such a seemingly insufficient weapon. Finally managing to kill the nutria, however, he removed it from the trap and brought the entire animal out of the marsh with him, showing it to Bill and Harley at the camp. Since the catch was made on a Saturday and the trappers would be going home that afternoon for church the following morning, Manson decided against removing the skin from the animal. Rather, he took the complete carcass home and placed it in his freezer where it would be preserved. Photographs were taken of the rodent and neighbors came to have a look at the huge rat. Thus was the first known catch of a nutria in the marshes of Chambers County.

During the 1950's, the nutria population spread like wildfire across the marshlands. The alligator population being at an all time low, the rodents really had no natural enemy in the marshes to control their numbers. They were a much hardier breed of rodent than the muskrat, dry and hot conditions never appearing to have an adverse affect on them. Their most notable features, however, were their feeding habits and rate of reproduction. The nutria seemed to eat all the time. Digging the roots of marsh vegetation from the muddy ground of the marshlands, they began their attack on the seacane. There was no regular breeding season for the nutria and they appeared to have two, and sometimes three, litters of young rats per year, each litter numbering from five to ten. Since no market had yet been established on the fur of the animals, the trappers did not take to the marshes after them, but did their best to avoid catching the nutria in their muskrat sets. Throughout the severe drought of the mid-1950's, conditions which both trappers and land owners hoped would stem the growth of the nutria population, the large rodents continued to increase in number.

By the latter part of the decade, the nutria had almost totally taken over the Chambers County marshlands. The whining sound of their voices could be heard from the lowlands day and night. Rather than build beds of their own, they often climbed atop the muskrat beds, sometimes three or four of them tramping about on the surface of the mounds. This proved to be too much commotion for the wild, but peace-loving muskrats, and the smaller rodents began leaving in tragic numbers, or simply interpreting the annoyance as another sign of "bad conditions" and refusing to reproduce. By the late 1950's, hardly a muskrat bed could be found in the Cove marshes.

The seacane and other marsh vegetation also suffered a terrible blow as the feasting by the hundreds of thousands of nutria went unabated. In all fairness, however, it must be noted that the blame for the destruction of the seacane during this period cannot be solely laid to the nutria. While the animals certainly did their part in cleaning the marshes of the valuable plant, the extensive salt water during the drought of 1956-57 also took a great toll on marshland vegetation. The nutria's entry into the marshes in great numbers just happened to coincide with the drought and the rodent is often unjustly blamed for all of the widespread disappearance of the vegetation.

During this period of the raging population of the nutria, Manson and his brothers, Bill and Vane, decided they had just as well catch a few of the nutria, cure their skins, and ship them to a fur buyer to see if any market existed on the nutria fur at all. They sent some two hundred large pelts to United Fur Brokers in New York City. Then began a long two-year wait for word about their furs. Finally, after having given up all hope of ever hearing from the brokers, a check came through the mail from United Fur. The brokers had found a buyer for their nutria and they were paid $2.65 per pelt for their catch.

Local Cove inhabitants worked feverishly to try to rid the marshes of the unwanted nutria. Although Manson and his brothers had sold one small lot of their furs, there was no indication that a ready market was anywhere in sight for large numbers of the nutria fur. When the mid-1950's drought ended, the rains became plentiful again and the Trinity River went on a rampage, flooding its banks and covering the marshlands with its muddy water. The nutria were flushed out of the lower areas of the marshes by the floodwaters and were seen perched atop every island, levee, log or any other object which protruded from the water. Area residents took to the marshes in droves, armed with .22 caliber rifles and hundreds of bullets in an all out attempt to kill out the nutria population. Hunters returned from the marshes with claims of having killed hundreds of nutria per day. Actually, many, if not most, of the nutria struck by .22 caliber bullets were not killed. The nutria must be shot directly in the head with small caliber bullets in order to cause their death in most cases. The majority of those hit in the bodies while swimming the bayous simply submerged, causing the riflemen to think they had killed the animals. Most of those shot in this manner rapidly recovered. This would be realized in later years as trappers who then sought the nutria furs for the market became aware of the amazing physical healing ability of the nutria. The nutria eventually became so thick that it was not uncommon to round a bend in a bayou with a boat and outboard motor and find a "herd" of fifteen to twenty of the animals swimming across the waterway.

As a final note on the trapping escapades of the 1950s, it might be mentioned that many people appear fascinated with the manner in which the professional fur trapper regards his occupation. For the trapper, the winter season is the finest part of any year. He does whatever he must to make a living during the hot months of summer, but always with his eye on the calendar, awaiting that grand day when he can turn the page to November and begin getting his equipment in condition so that he will be ready when those first cold northers begin pushing their way southward across the coastal marshlands. To the trapper, the matter of making his sets in the marshes is more than just a way of making a living for his family; it becomes an obsession. It is almost as if he has marsh mud in his veins. He works throughout the day making some fresh sets in new territory. Retiring for the night, he can hardly sleep a wink due to the anticipation of getting out and running the trapline at daylight the next morning. And, during the months when he is not trapping, he talks about trapping – with anyone who will listen. His favorite summer pastime is getting together with two or three fellow trappers and exchanging tales of experiences on the trapline. To him, the natural beauty of the raw, freshly-cured animal fur is much more attractive than the finished product in a woman's coat, although he is too much of a gentleman of the "old school" to tell the lady so. One of the best examples of a Cove man who truly had "trapping in the blood" was the case of Dorris Dutton, who lived on the banks of Cotton Bayou. During the summer, he farmed cotton for a living, but during the winter he trapped muskrats as a way of life. Shortly before passing from this life in December 1958, he reportedly told some visiting neighbors: "What I dread most about dying is that I won't ever be able to trap muskrats again." What words could better describe the outlook of a fur trapper?

■　■　■　■　■　■　■

In 1959, Hurricane "Debra" crossed the Gulf of Mexico and aimed her punch at the upper Texas coast. She was not a major hurricane, her winds not far in excess of one hundred miles per hour, but as the eye of the storm crossed the coastline near Baytown, the Cove area found itself just to the east of the center which, historically, is the most powerful sector of a tropical cyclone.

Manson's principle concern during this storm was his thirty-five-foot shrimpboat, the "Freda." Anchoring her in a section of his boat landing which had been dug especially to accommodate the large craft, she was moored, bow and stern, with lengths of the new polyethylene rope some one inch in diameter, giving the ropes plenty of slack so that the vessel would be at liberty to rise with the expected incoming tides. It was hoped that a large dump, or mound of earth, some ten to twelve feet in height on the bank to her south side would deflect most of the wind, waves and debris from her wooden hull.

After several hours of the powerful winds buffeting the coast, Manson decided he had to go to the boat landing about daylight to check on how the "Freda" was managing. What he saw gave him a start. The boat had broken loose from its moorings, having pulled the pilings from the ground as the wind applied such great pressure against the vessel. "Freda" had washed across the boat slip and rested aground on top of another earthen dump, some twelve feet in height, on the northeast side of the landing. Already the logs and debris were beginning to pile up against the south side of the boat's hull and Manson knew it was only a matter of time before one of the crashing logs drove a hole through her side. In addition to that worry, he knew that when the storm winds began to slacken, the tides would begin to recede from the dump, leaving the boat perched atop the narrow-peaked mound, from which point she would likely roll to her side down the decline of the dump and probably turn upside down in the water of the boat landing. Something had to be done quickly.

Manson, his son, Kendon, and his nephew, James "Jamie" Hoffman, the latter of whom resided at the old Joe Maley place on the hillside overlooking the landing, waded their way through chest deep water where hours before had existed dry land, and reached the stranded vessel. Climbing aboard, they took up poles with which to keep the incoming logs pushed off the side of the boat in efforts to save her hull from damage. As the winds began to lessen during the morning and the tide slowly receded, the trio pried against the north side of the boat, slowly moving her great weight down the side of the mound as the waters gradually fell. After some six to eight hours of the exerting work, the water was back within the confines of the boat slip and the "Freda" boat rested safely upon the surface of the water.

After this experience, Manson made up his mind that if he ever managed to get the large vessel out of the slip and into open water, he would not be the owner of the boat the next time a hurricane threatened the area. But, before anything could be moved out the boat slip and onto Cotton Lake, the landing had to be cleared of the logs, wreckage and debris which floated on the surface from the foot of the hillside to a point almost halfway to the lakeshore. Manson recalled the tiring work he had put in with the identical job ten years earlier after the storm of 1949, and dreaded another thirty days of similar back-breaking work. But, it would be different this time. Several members of the Clark and Maley families now used the landing as a dock for their boats. And, in 1949, they had seen that it was possible to clean up the mess as Manson labored alone on that occasion. The storm winds had hardly diminished back to normal daily velocity when help began arriving. After a period of a week, the boat landing was again open to Cotton Lake.

Manson made good his promise to himself not to own the shrimpboat "Freda" the next time a hurricane struck the region. Within weeks after freeing her from the debris of Hurricane "Debra," he sold the boat to Orville Bagent and Vernon Kemp of Barbers Hill. It was a decision which, two years later, he would be grateful he had made.

▪ CHAPTER VII ▪

THE 1960's

Weatherwise, the decade of the 1960's came in much like the '50's had gone out– like a raging lion. During the winter of 1960, following the end of the duck hunting season, Manson was trotline fishing on Cotton Lake and had lines with a combined total of hundreds of hooks scattered all over the lake, many of them anchored on one end to the frames of his duck blinds.

A massive blast of cold air came rushing southward in the form of a blue norther, having had its origin in the frozen wastelands of the Arctic region. Temperatures plunged to well below the freezing mark and remained so for several days, forming a solid sheet of ice on Cotton Lake almost one inch thick from shore to shore. The lake remained frozen for some three days and nights.

On the following Friday morning, there began a noticeable rise in the temperature and by noon the mercury had risen above the freezing point. The norther was losing its grip and the wind gradually began to shift to the northeast. During the afternoon, the wind went around directly from the east, rapidly increasing in velocity. The ice, still covering the lake, but no longer held securely to the shores by the freezing temperatures, began to move with the increasing easterly winds like a great sheet of glass. Having thawed to a thickness over most of the surface of a half inch, the lake of ice cut down everything in its path at water level as it continued its slow, but incessant move toward the west end of the lake. The air was rent with the crumpling reverberations of breaking ice as jagged cracks worked their way across the frozen surface, much like lightning bolts from a threatening sky. The ice piled up on the bluffs overlooking Ernest Cove in the west corner of the lake, reaching a height of ten to fifteen feet at certain points. It was a sight which people of the semi-tropical Texas coast rarely have an opportunity to observe.

With the ice driven from the lake by the easterly wind, white-capped waves replaced the frozen sheet. The lake suddenly had an eerie appearance. Where the frames of duck blinds and the spindly poles of trotlines had risen from the water only hours before, the surface of the lake was now unobstructed from shore to shore. The ice had sliced down everything that had jutted above the water. The next fall would be a busy season with the complete rebuilding of the duck blinds required prior to the opening day of the hunting season, and there would be a great deal of expense involved in replacing all the lost trotlines. But, such was part of the price for making one's living from nature. There were no government programs ready to provide subsidies, no unions to protest the plight of the marshman when he was dealt with harshly. But, such was the way he liked it. Anything otherwise would make him less of an individual and more of a proletariat slave. Freedom comes packaged in the ability of a man to earn what he can, but to also take the setbacks as part of a day's work. If a man is to expect the right to succeed, he must also be willing to accept the responsibility of the lean times. Indeed, a form of governmental subsidy designed to bolster the sagging fur market years before had been abandoned in large part due to fur trappers throughout the nation who did not want government tampering with their business.

During the 1950's, something had taken place in Chambers County which during the following years would change the lifestyle of the region to a greater extent than almost anyone had dared to imagine. Interstate Highway 10 was completed across the county from east to west. Huge bridges now spanned the Trinity, Old and Lost rivers. The highway cut its path across the northern portion of Cove. Only a few had the foresight to realize that this spelled the beginning of the end of the quiet way of life in Cove which most of its inhabitants had merely assumed would always be the rule. The region was now open to the world and it would not take the world many years to find it. For a while, however, things remained fairly quiet. A strange vehicle might pass through the community from time to time, watched suspiciously by area natives, but an individual could still take to the marshes where if he saw anyone, it was likely to be one of his neighbors.

■ ■ ■ ■ ■ ■ ■

In September 1961, nature again went on a rampage. A hurricane named "Carla" found its way through the channel between Cuba and the Yucatan Peninsula and launched itself into the Gulf of Mexico. For days, coastal residents monitored the storm's progress across the Gulf, listening to advisories on the radio and television. Newsmen forecasted this storm to be rapidly growing into killer proportions. The size of the hurricane, almost five hundred miles in diameter, was certain to affect a great portion of the coast regardless of where her center made landfall.

With the storm still a couple of days out in the Gulf, Manson began to take some preventative measures against her destructive power. At his landing, he towed several boats from the water's edge to a point up the hillside at about a fifteen-foot elevation where he felt they would be safe from the potential of rising tides. Then, he remembered an old friend on Cedar Island near the mouth of Cross Bayou at Trinity Bay.

Rudolph Krajka was a Bohemian man who worked as caretaker for the hunting lodge of C. B. Delhomme. He had remained on the island two years earlier during Hurricane "Debra" and had been forced into the second story of the old woodframe house by the rising tide water into the structure. During the two-year interim since that storm, Delhomme had constructed a new house on the island, an $80,000 showplace where he hoped to take his business associates for hunting and lodging during the coming duck season. The new single-story building had only been completed for some two months when "Carla" appeared in the Gulf. Since the old wooden structure had withstood the pounding of "Debra" two years earlier, it was hoped that this new stone structure would likewise stand up to the onslaught of "Carla."

Manson and Kendon went to the island by boat and assisted Rudolph in securing things about the place. They also intended to persuade him to leave the island before the storm struck. When Manson mentioned helping the caretaker and his wife to get things ready to get out of the marshes, the Bohemian grinned and replied, "I ain't going nowhere. I'll get up in the attic and be okay." Manson told Rudolph that "Carla" could not be compared to "Debra" in potential strength, that this storm was now packing winds of over 140 miles per hour. Still, Rudolph persisted and, in his broken English said he would need to remain on the island "to take care of things."

While Manson argued the point with Rudolph, he thought about Sol Wilburn who lived in a small house on a similar island on Reds Bayou. Surely, Sol had already left. He knew what these storms could do. In fact, he had been washed out of the marshes during "Debra", managing to keep his boat upright until it was hurled upon the bluffs overlooking Cotton Lake near Ernest Cove. To be on the safe side, however, Manson sent Kendon in his boat to Sol's place to make sure the man had left, or was preparing to do so. Kendon found Sol in his little cabin, trying to get his battery radio to work. Asked if he had heard about the storm, the elderly man replied, "No, my radio's been broke, but I thought there must be something in the Gulf the way this weather's been acting the past couple of days." Learning from his visitor of the type of hurricane now bearing down upon the coast, Sol wasted no time in gathering some clothing and other articles. Walking to the bayou, he climbed in his skiff and headed for the highland.

Back on Cedar Island, Manson and Rudolph were still arguing about the latter's need to get out of the marsh. At about that time, a small yacht came around the nearest bend in Cross Bayou, appearing very much out of place in the wilderness of the marshlands, and docked in front of the island. A man in a necktie, business suit, and street hat stepped onto the bayou bank and walked toward them. The man was C. B. Delhomme, the wealthy but easy-going owner of the lodge, who had come to the marsh from Houston to make certain Rudolph left for safety. "Well, it looks like everything is taken care of here. Rudolph, are you ready to leave?" "I ain't goin' nowhere," repeated the caretaker. Manson told Delhomme of his unsuccessful attempt to talk the aging man into leaving the marsh and that if he (Delhomme) could not persuade him to leave, this might be the last time they would see him alive.

Delhomme informed the men he had just heard on his boat radio that the hurricane's winds were now in excess of 150 miles per hour and continuing to increase by the hour. "The whole Gulf will be pouring over this island tomorrow or the next day and I don't want to have to worry about you down here in the marsh." The stubborn Bohemian repeated his intention of staying on to care for the place. Delhomme then informed Rudolph that if he had to fire him from his job in order to get him off the island, he would do just that. This uncharacteristic threat of unemployment from his normally mild-mannered boss drove the story home to the caretaker. He was gone as darkness fell over the marsh.

"Carla" stalled in the Gulf as if trying to decide where to deliver her deadly blow. With peak winds now between 160 and 170 miles per hour, the area which received her center was certain to be wiped out. Her tremendous size would ensure death and destruction along much of the Texas coastline. Slowly, she set her sights on the Port O'Connor/Port Lavaca area down the coast from Galveston, just north of Corpus Christi. As the great mass of wind and rain began to near the land, she stalled again just offshore, mercilessly hammering the Texas coast, as well as that of southwestern Louisiana, for three days and nights. The Cove area received winds of well in excess of 100 miles per hour. On the final night of the storm, "Carla" finally moved inland, bringing the massive tides she had pushed across the Gulf. Electrical power lines fell before her mighty winds as did thousands of homes along the coast.

Manson's family was abruptly stirred from their sleep at about 2:00 AM to the sound of a large hackberry tree uprooting at one corner of the house and falling across the gully behind the structure. The house itself shivered under the impact of the wind. Manson decided to go to the boat landing to see what was happening on the waterfront. He, Myra and Kendon all climbed inside the pickup truck and began the slow drive toward the landing. Several cottonmouth moccasins were observed on the road, having been flushed from the marshes by the high tides. Nearing the old Zack Maley place, they found a telephone wire across the road, about three feet above the ground. Kendon severed the obstruction with a pair of pliers.

In the lower woods along Spring Branch Gully, they could see the water pushing ever higher against the highland as the dark waves crashed among the elm and hackberry trees of the woods. Finally reaching the landing, Manson discovered that some of the boats he had pulled partway up the hillside had not been towed far enough. The water and waves had reached a point as to claim four of the skiffs, totally destroying them. The wind had managed to blow beneath another, lifting it from the ground, and sent it rolling across the field, beating its hull to pieces. A utility building below the hillside at the landing was now being crushed by the logs and debris driven ashore by the wind and water.

By the late afternoon of the third day of the storm, "Carla" had finally moved inland and raced northward, spending her remaining fury by breaking up into rainsqualls over interior parts of Texas. The coast was a wreck.

Rudolph Krajka came to Manson's home and Manson offered to take him to his home at the lodge on Cedar Island. Arriving at the Cross Bayou estate, they found the wreckage almost unbelievable. The large six-bedroom stone house had been thoroughly gutted, with only a portion of the north wall remaining. About fifty nutria sat perched atop what was left of part of the roof. The smaller quarters of the caretaker was seen lying on its side in the marsh north of the island. Rudolph was now glad that his friend and his employer had made him leave the island.

Back at Manson's boat landing, the debris was piled two to three feet thick along the bank and edge of the hillside. This time the tide had risen to such a great height that the tangled mass of wreckage was all deposited on the highland rather than upon the waters of the boat slip. The cleanup process would require only the burning of the debris on the land. Manson thought about a certain spot at the old Zack Maley place where he remembered the high point of the tide having reached during the great 1915 hurricane when he was a boy. Driving to the old homesite, he found that the high edge of the driftline of debris had reached the exact same point during "Carla."

"Carla" had accomplished a feat which area residents had attempted to perform for nearly a decade. She had almost wiped out the nutria population in the Cove marshes. After a couple of days of hot sun following the storm, the stench of the decaying animal bodies beneath the drift filled the air with its putrid odor. Never again would the nutria be allowed to reach an uncontrollable point in population as had been the case during the 1950's. Within three years after Hurricane "Carla" the big fur houses up north began experimenting with uses for nutria fur and trappers went to the marshes with this incentive of keeping the rodents under control with steel traps.

■　■　■　■　■　■　■

During the 1960's, more people began to learn of the marshlands of Cove. Strange faces began appearing in the marshes. Now and then, Manson would take some of his hunters to a duck blind on Cotton Lake only to discover that some "outsider" had already occupied the blind. During some of these first such occurrences, he allowed the intruders to go ahead and hunt the blind that morning and took his hunters elsewhere. But, as such flagrant displays of trespassing became more frequent year after year, he grew more and more impatient with the encroachers as he had to put them out of his blinds in order to allow his paying hunters to enter.

With the exception of the several regular hunters who had frequented Manson's guide service for many years, the quality of those who came to make their hunts on Cotton Lake deteriorated noticeably during this period. They were a different type of people. Many seemed unwilling, or unable, to do anything for themselves. Manson took to calling many of them "babies" due to their manner of expecting everything to be done for them. The number of those who seemed only to want to shoot their guns increased dramatically. While most of the oldtime hunters realized and accepted the fact that there were going to be days when few or no ducks would be on the move to provide shooting on the lake, some of this new breed became verbally hostile after such unsuccessful days. Some were found shooting at mullet as they jumped from the lake waters while others fired at seagulls or any other bird which flew across the lake. Manson summed up these people with the observation, "It's getting to where there are just not any hunters anymore. They are nothing but shooters."

One of the greatest impediments to the duck hunting guide business on Cotton Lake had always been the low tides which occurred during strong, windy northers. At such times there was simply not enough water left in the lake to operate an outboard motor in towing the hunting skiffs to the blinds. Much too often these periods of low tide would coincide with the arrival of a "full house" of hunters, all eager to be on the way to the blinds. Upon discovering that the water was too low to navigate, the fees were returned to the hunters with an apology for not being able to carry out the day's hunt.

During the early and mid-1960's, Manson decided to try something which several people had suggested as a possible answer to the low tide dilemma. He purchased a small airplane engine, had it mounted on the stern of a flat bottomed boat, and used this rig to tow the hunters to and from the blinds during low water periods. He did not like the noise the engine and propeller put forth, but at least he could navigate in low tide. The hunters found it a frigid experience to sit in the skiffs behind the wind-propelled craft and would invariably turn their backs to the freezing wind being blown across them.

Manson used the boat on an average of only a couple of days per week, depending upon how long a period of low tide continued. When a norther played itself out and the tide began returning to the lake, he retired the noisy craft and gladly went back to using his outboard rig. After a while, he began to detect a change for the worst in the hunting on Cotton Lake. The ducks simply were not coming to the lake in the numbers that had always been the case before. He noted that for several days after he used the airboat on the lake, even for brief periods, the duck kills on the lake were decidedly down in number. Eventually, he completely retired the airboat for good, reasoning that the convenience of being able to operate on the lake even during the lowest of tides was not worth the negative effect the noise was obviously having on the duck population. As he suspended his own use of the airboat, the only one then operating in the Cove area, little did he realize that others, those whom he had come to view merely as "shooters" rather than hunters, would soon begin using factory-made airboats and would exhibit little or no obvious regard for the effect of the noise on the wildlife of the area.

■　■　■　■　■　■　■

Hurricane "Carla" had completely destroyed the camp which Manson and his companions had used in the south central Chambers County marshes since the early 1940's. The camphouse was gone with all the furnishings and equipment. They considered building a new camphouse in the Wilborn Ranch marshes, but learned that the storm's destruction in that area had been so complete as to kill practically every animal in the region. Manson, therefore, returned to full time trapping and hunting in the Cove area marshlands.

■ CLARK'S DUCK HUNTING SERVICE ■

Owned and Operated By Manson L. Clark 1921 - 1973

The map of Cotton Lake on the opposite page indicates the locations of Clark's duck blinds as they were situated in 1960. The locations are basically the same as they had been for many preceding years as well as in the few subsequent seasons. Following are the names of the blinds as many of Clark's hunters learned to refer to them. Numbers to the left of the names of the blinds correspond with the numbered blind locations on the map.

1. 2nd Ernest Cove Blind
2. 1st Ernest Cove Blind
3. 1st Middle Blind
4. Hadaway Blind
5. 1st Mullet Slough Blind
6. 2nd Mullet Slough Blind
7. Mullet Slough Blind
8. Bayou Blind (or George Wilburn Blind)
9. Horse Island Blind
10. Middle Blind
11. West Middle Blind
12. Cotton Bayou Point Blind
13. Gougee Bayou Cove Blind
14. Leo Blind
15. Mitchell Blind
16. Harry Blind
17. Basil Blind
18. Thurman Blind
19. Harley Blind
20. Jamie Blind

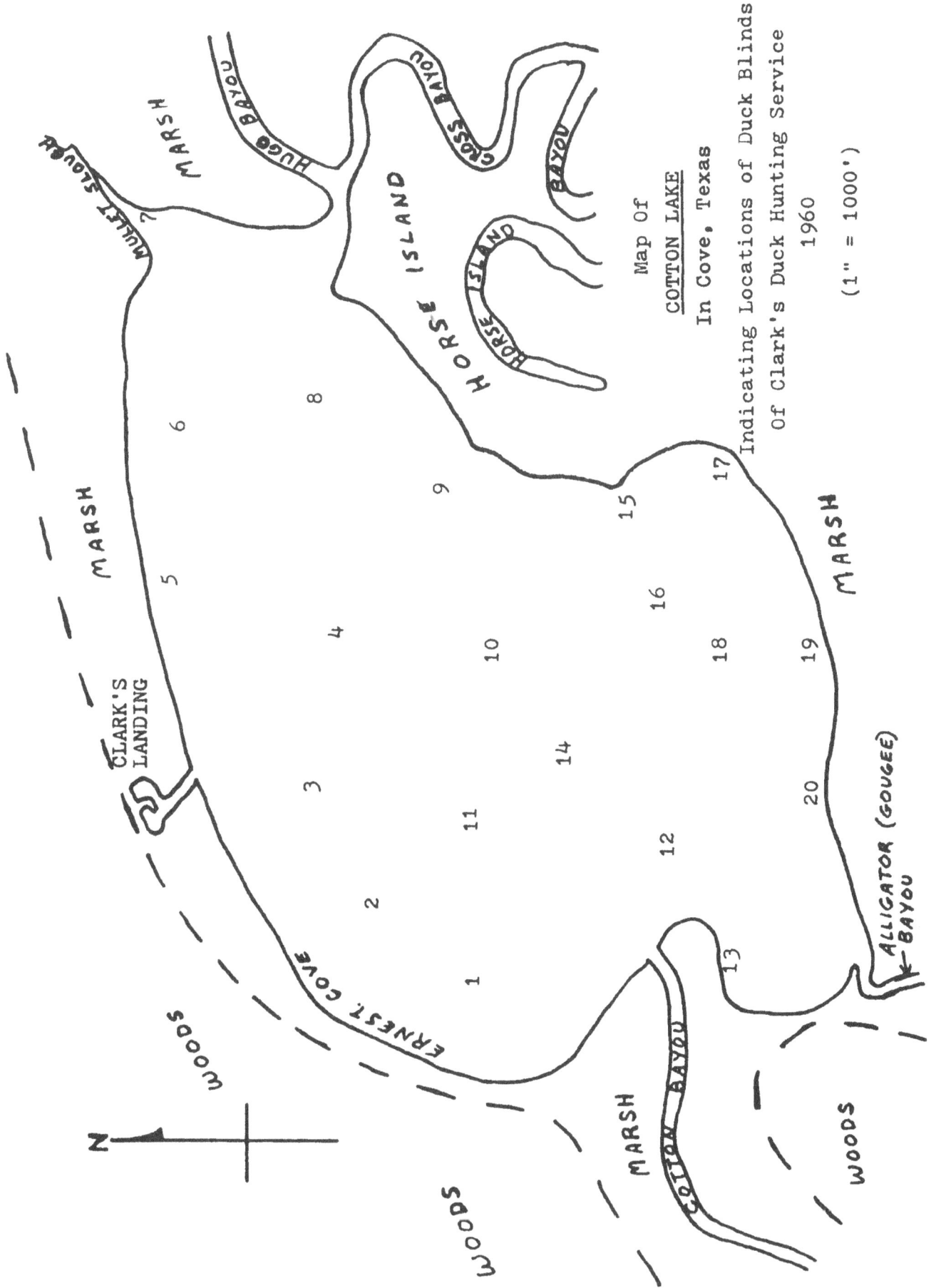

Map Of
COTTON LAKE
In Cove, Texas

Indicating Locations of Duck Blinds
Of Clark's Duck Hunting Service
1960

(1" = 1000')

CHAPTER VIII

1970 - 1982

Cove was undergoing drastic changes. New people were moving into the area. Manson could understand why people would want to purchase land in Cove. He was a lover of the land and always believed that even if a man lost everything else he owned, he could remain afloat in this life if he had a few acres of land. He once remarked, "I intend to hold onto my property as long as I can scratch together enough nickels and dimes to pay my taxes." But he also realized that difficult financial times were in the making. While abnormally high fur prices came in very handy during the early and mid-1970's, he saw in it a foreboding of things to come. The last time he had seen the market behave in such a manner was during the late 1920's, on the eve of the Great Depression.

Most of the new folks who were moving into Cove proved to be good neighbors. The majority accepted Cove's old, ingrained way of life, even the clannish nature of the descendants of the old pioneer families of the region. Those who were sincere in their desire to become accepted as a part of the community realized it might take time to win the complete confidence and trust of their neighbors.

While few problems were encountered by the Cove natives from those who had come to Cove to make their home, the real problems came in the form of those from surrounding areas who found Cove to be a place in which to perform their devilish deeds. Theft increased substantially during the early 1970's. Manson and Kendon had been keeping their boats docked at the old Zack Maley place. One morning in late November 1972, they went to the landing to begin running their traplines for the day and discovered that both their outboard motors had been stolen during the night. Other such thefts were recorded in the community, with outboard motors being one of the primary targets of the thieves.

In early 1975, Chambers County purchased part of the old Zack Maley property and opened the boat landing there as a public facility. The stage was set for the complete undoing of the lifestyle of the men who had always made their livelihoods from the marshes. With the increased boat traffic across Cotton Lake from the public landing, it was no longer possible for Manson to continue operation of his duck hunting guide service. After fifty-two years in the business, he was forced to close the service the following season. Something which some prefer to call "progress" had caught up with Cove. If the local people believed that the problems they had encountered from the acts of strangers during the past ten years were serious, those past problems now took on more the form of a picnic. As more and more outsiders found the location of the boat landing, the local people were pushed farther and farther to the rear of their community. No matter that the only route by which to reach the landing was a half-mile-long road across private property of several landowners; the public had to have its access. The taxpaying landowner now became a second class citizen. His voice was not as loud as that of the invader. The facility came to be known among some local Cove people as "the welfare center" due to the large number of people who appeared to prefer such free government services as opposed to going elsewhere where they had to pay their own way.

In 1975, while cleaning a mess of catfish at one of his outbuildings, Manson underwent the effects of a severe stroke. Admitted to a Houston hospital for an extended period of time, he regained his health and again went to the marshes the following winter to work his traplines.

At seventy years of age, he refused offers from longtime fellow trappers that he take some of their territory with easier access in exchange for some of his rougher trapping grounds. His view was that if a man intended to be a fur trapper, he had to make do with what he had. However, some of that which he had was now being taken from him as, indeed, it was from most of the other trappers of the region. Among the strangers who had found the Cove marshes in recent years were a number of unscrupulous characters to whom theft was a supplemental business. The trapper could no longer mark the location of his sets, because the trap thief would find them first. Some believed that a growing nationwide movement to stop the trapping of furbearers provided some of the thieves with an incentive to carry on their scavenging of the marshlands. Others did not steal, but rather approached traps which held animals awaiting the trapper's arrival, and poured a shotgun blast into the animal, rendering the furbearer's skin totally worthless.

Serious duck hunting was rapidly becoming a thing of the past in the Cove marshes. If the single homemade airboat that Manson had used occasionally during periods of low tide on Cotton Lake in the 1960's had affected the hunting there until he quit using the noisy craft, dozens of the more powerful and more noisy water vehicles now provided a constant roar in the marshes. Areas deep in the lowlands which once could be reached only by an occasional hunter who was willing to make the difficult trek on foot could now be reached with an airboat, leaving the waterfowl no places where they might seek refuge for rest. The gutting of the marshlands was well underway.

Manson's older brother and lifelong companion in the marshes, Bill, suffered a heart attack on March 15, 1972, while running a trotline on Trinity Bay. Discovered by neighbors Chuck and Dennis Peting, he was rushed to the Cove highland and from there taken to a hospital in Dayton, where he passed away later that evening. It is somewhat ironic to note that the death of the seventy-one-year-old fur trapper came on the closing day of muskrat season that year. Like his brothers and others who had trapped and fished the region, he had participated in the "golden age" of the Cove marshlands during the first half century of his life.

Many of the other men of Cove and other sections of Chambers County who, like Manson Clark, have made their livelihoods from the fruits of the Creator have also passed from this life. His old friend and salty seaman Saylus "Sails" Elliott has been gone for many years. Morgan LaFour of Wallisville, who guided duck hunters on Lake Charlotte for as many years as did Manson on Cotton Lake, had continued in his business until failing eyesight finally caught up with him prior to his death. The hard-bitten humor of Nesbit "Whop-down" Dunman, also of Wallisville, was uncompromising to the end on the matter of the impending takeover by the so-called sportsmen, but was finally driven from making his livelihood on the Trinity River as his hoop nets, one by one, were stolen or mutilated, and his trotlines cut loose from their poles and left to be swept down the river. Dorris Dutton, lifelong resident of the Cotton Bayou region of Cove, expressed his love for the trapping business shortly before his death. Manson's brother-in-law, Harley Maley, spent his entire life on the north shore of Cotton Lake, and passed away on September 1, 1982. At his funeral services, Gerald Winslow, officiating over the services, pretty well summed up Harley's life as well as those of the other men who have spent their lives at their work in the marshes, bayous and bays of the region: "Harley Maley was one of those men who spent his life with nature, one of those of a free and independent spirit who has lived a life that lesser men have been afraid to try. A few of his breed still remain with us, but when they have all gone, with them will have gone an era. They are the real pioneer stock of our people."

Those who do remain hold memories which neither the government nor the invading hordes can take away from them. In Cove, men like Manson Clark, Linzie Griffith,

Arnold McKay, Vane Clark, Gene Dutton and others enjoy getting together to recount the way things used to be, when there was always work to be done in the marshes, when the only scavenger on the trapline might be an old, hungry coon out looking for an easy meal. For all practical purposes, the shrimping, crabbing and oystering are all gone, as is the alligator hunting. A man might kill a duck or two now and then if he is fortunate enough to locate a secluded spot away from the ravages of the airboats; he might catch a mess of catfish if his trotlines are left alone for a couple of nights; he can even catch a few nutria, and maybe a muskrat or two, providing the thieves are not successful in locating his trapline. But, the "old days" are the usual topics of their discussions, the days when the marshlands lay quiet and undisturbed, when a man could get away to himself and be alone with his Maker.

In late 1975, just before Christmas, a telephone call came from Houston television station KPRC, an affiliate of the NBC television network. The caller said he had been referred to the Clarks by Beaumont fur buyer J. H. Welborn as a possible source of acquiring some pictures of raw fur pelts. Manson told the man to come ahead and take his photos. Within a couple hours two men arrived, one of whom conducted an interview with Manson and his son while the other took moving pictures of them in the process of caring for the hides. The men displayed a desire to come back during the week between Christmas and New Years Day to accompany one of the trappers on the trapline. Both Manson and Kendon pointed out that their boats would accommodate only one passenger at a time, so one of the men, Gary James, said he would come alone. Manson's trapline being farther into the marshes than Kendon's at that time, James decided to go with Kendon for the trapline filming, because this route would enable him to return to Houston earlier.

It was a cold, drizzly Thursday morning at daylight when the television man arrived and he and Kendon left the landing. James wore only a light wind breaker over his clothes and Kendon attempted to persuade him to wear one of his heavier coats as the chill on the water would be much more severe than on the high land. The man said he would be fine, but after some half hour in the boat, buffeted by the chilling north wind, the man began to evince a distinct alteration in his skin color. Still, Gary James persevered and got his film footage. Finishing one section of the trapline, Kendon told the man he still had another line of traps to run in the marshes south of Cotton Lake, but that if he (James) was getting too cold, he would take him back to the high land before going to those traps. The man quickly indicated that he was sure he had enough film for what was needed and the boat headed inland against the north wind.

101

After consuming hot cups of coffee, the man's natural skin color began to return to his face. Upon his departure for the return trip to Houston, Gary James told the Clarks to watch "The Eyes of Texas" on KPRC the following Saturday evening if they wanted to see the results of the filming. This was their first indication of what was to be done with the film. They had been under the impression that a study of the fur industry was afoot and that the television station had only needed some shots of actual raw furs to add to the study. And, here they were, about to be displayed on a Statewide television program. Somewhat dubious about the prospect, they told only immediate family members and some local Cove trappers to watch "The Eyes of Texas" that Saturday night, but did not even tell some of them what they might expect to see.

It was a long and nerve-wracking two-day wait for the Saturday evening program. They thought of every possibility they could imagine regarding the manner in which the film might be presented. They were aware that television programs were often slanted in such a manner as to create public opinion about certain people or their lifestyles. Would the film be so edited as to cast them into the roles of ruthless and cruel men, out to make a dollar through inhumane treatment of wild animals? Such was the view that the antitrapping movement throughout the country had been trying to convey to the public through numerous devious means, and it might be that Channel 2 TV in Houston was in cahoots with those characters. As the time for the viewing arrived, however, they were pleased to see that the program presented an unbiased view of the trapping business.

During the following April of 1976, *The Baytown Sun* newspaper, in a follow up article on the television program, sent reporter Mrs. Betsy Webber to Cove to interview the trappers and write a story. The article appeared in the April 28 edition, after the trapping season had ended for the year. An increased number of people from outside the Cove area began showing up in the Cove marshes during the next couple years, attempting to move into the trapping territories of some of the old trapping families. Confrontations arose over such usurpation of longstanding trapping rights. Realizing the possibility that news coverage of the trapping business in the area might have had its share of influence in the matter, the Clarks refused future requests for news coverage of their marshland activities. Stating that they had almost been "publicized out of business," the reporters accepted the explanation as a logical reason for their refusal to allow any more publicity and the requests finally stopped coming.

■ ■ ■ ■ ■ ■ ■

Manson Clark had been pleased that alligator hunting was outlawed during the late 1950's. The law allowed the once numerous reptiles to stave off eventual extinction in the marshes and to increase their number to some extent from their low ebb in population during the previously mentioned decade. But, when others spoke of the "great numbers" of alligators later inhabiting the marshes, Manson was amused. Those making excursions down the five or six-mile length of Cross Bayou from Cotton Lake to Trinity Bay often returned with stories of "alligators lying everywhere." Pressed to relate the number of alligators they actually saw on the trip, the number was usually less than a dozen. While Manson dreaded the possible reopening of an alligator hunting season, especially on the west side of Chambers County, because of his fear that they would again be killed out, he often smiled and recalled:

"When you can stand in your tracks on a bayou bank in the marsh and count twenty-five 'gator heads in the bayou in front of you, then you can say there are a lot of 'gators again." Manson Clark had done just that during the Golden Age of the Cove, Texas marshlands.

• CHAPTER IX •

THE MARSHMANS JOURNAL

(EDITOR'S NOTE – Following are various accounts of wildlife experiences by the subject of this sketch, Manson L. Clark, as related in his journals and notes which were written and recorded by him for some four decades. Some of these stories and anecdotes are mentioned in the preceeding accounts in this volume, while others are not. Some are indepth accounts while others are related in only a sentence or two. The original author of the journals and notes wrote with the knowledge derived from a lifetime of experience and he has written of those things about which he is most familiar. Little time or space has been devoted to description of people or places.

There has been very little editing of the following notes, and then only such editing where it was considered necessary for the clarification of various points. Minor corrections have been made in spelling and punctuation. Aside from such editing, the entries here are verbatim.

The notes presented here, almost directly from the hand of Manson Clark, are entered without regard for chronological sequence or strict adherence to "the King's English." It is a collection of events which have been a part of the outdoor life and experiences of the subject of this sketch.)

• First Alligator Hunt •

In 1919, I bought a Bulls Eye headlight from Sears Roebuck when I was 15 years old. Went on my first hunt by myself down Alligator Bayou, now called Gougee Bayou, with a single barrel shotgun, 12 gauge. Alligators were plentiful in those days. I went down about a quarter of a mile in the bayou about sundown and when dark came I lit up the old Bulls Eye which burns signal oil, and shot 15 'gators before I found I could get close up to them by blinding them with the light, and killed the last five by getting close. Shot 20 'gators on the way back. All the shells I had. Skins ran then from 75¢ to $1.25 for 7-foot to 12-foot hides. Sold the skins to old George King who bought hides at that time. In those days we didn't have to pole hunt 'gators; could get plenty around the lakes and bayous.

▪ Early Duck Hunting ▪

I shot ducks with a single barrel shotgun. One day I got 40 ducks back of The Ridge with 33 shells. In those days I carried duck hunters back in the marshes when 25 and 50 was the daily limit on ducks.

▪ Some Alligator Totals and Prices ▪

Things rocked on with wildlife hunting and fishing until about 1927 when things began to tighten up. Had to go out in the marshes to get many big 'gators. In 1929, we had an awful rise in the river. I could run my boat all over the marsh. I got 228 alligators in June 1929, all over 7 foot long. They were worth $4.50 and down in 1930-31. In 1932-33, things were tight. A big 'gator skin would bring only $2.25, and they had begun to get scarce.

▪ Muskrat Prices ▪

The high water that came in 1920 stayed up high for 3 months and killed out the muskrats, but in 1933-34 they started to get thick again. In 1931-32, tops [large, Number One grade furs] brought 20¢ and 25¢ each. In 1933-34, they went from 40¢ to 70¢. In 1934-35, we got 80¢ for tops at the last of the season. I caught 1,300 'rats that year.

▪ A Stubborn Alligator ▪

In 1928, I was pole hunting one day in the high seacane about a mile from my boat when I heard a big noise about fifty feet from me. It was an 11-foot 'gator crawling from a hole. I only had one shell, had shot the others I had with me at other 'gators. I got up pretty close and let him have it in the eye. He acted like he was dead, so I punched him with the iron rod that I used to punch them out of the holes with, and he came at me and like to have got me. So I had to walk all the way back to the boat to get some more shells, and when I got back to where he had been he was gone. I trailed him about 3 or 4 hundred yards. He heard me coming and lay still. As I went to shoot him, he came at me again, but this time I was watching and I let him have it. It was getting dark by the time I got him skinned and back to the boat. At that time it was nothing to get 4 or 5 big 'gators in a day.

▪ Matagorda County 'Gators ▪

Back in 1928, I hunted a swamp near Bay City. These 'gators had never been hunted. Charles Joseph was with me on that hunt. We had a pole with a hook on each side and pulled out two five-foot 'gators at one time, one on each hook. We killed 17 'gators that one evening and barely got them skinned when it started raining. It rained all night. There were plenty of cottonmouth moccasins in that country, and nigras too.

▪ Another Close Call ▪

Bill [Clark] and me were trailing a ten-foot alligator in the marsh one day, and I stepped across a slough about 3 feet wide. The 'gator was laying in it and slapped at me as I stepped over. I got my gun and grunted at the 'gator. He stuck his head up and I got him.

▪ The Nature of the Beast ▪

Big alligators can be very dangerous if you try to get too smart with them. Many times I have had them to grab my hook pole and drag it twenty feet back in the ground with such power that a man would be as easy for him to drag back into the ground and tear him to pieces. The older they are, the stronger they are. I have had them to shake the ground for 15 or 20 feet around when I touched them with the iron rod. Most large 'gators live and den up in marshes and never come out to open water. The female 'gator builds a nest out of grass, mud and sticks about 2 or 3 feet high and from 3 to 5 feet across, and lays from 30 to 60 eggs down in the center of the nest. The eggs will not hatch if she hasn't been with the male 'gator to fertilize the eggs. She generally has a hole of water close to the nest about 3 or 4 feet across and from 7 to 12 feet deep, but not straight down, about 3 to 5 feet under the ground. In all 'gator holes, the back end of the tunnel has a turning basin. They crawl in and go back to the end of the hole and turn around, then always come out of the hole headfirst. Sometimes they lay with their head at the edge of the pit and the instant anything falls within reach, they grab it and drag it back into the hole and tear it to pieces. The female 'gator rarely gets much above 9 feet long, but a very few reach 10 to 12 feet. I have killed a lot of 10, 11 and 12-foot male 'gators, but have only killed 6 over thirteen feet long out of about 2,000. My largest one was fourteen feet and eight inches long. I believe that's about as large as they get, at least in this area. 42 alligators is the most I have ever killed in one night's hunt. That was in the Willow Marsh Ditch in 1942.

▪ Stephenson Lake 'Gators ▪

I also killed several alligators in Stephenson Lake which is near Smith Point. Owen Maley and I hunted those 'gators there and killed only the big ones. We would pull them out of the hole and chop them in the back of the head with a hatchet. One night while hunting in Stephenson Lake, we saw a 'gator out on the bank after a skunk. He was almost up to the polecat, about 20 feet from the edge of the water. All at once the skunk sprayed the 'gator squarely in the face and the alligator turned and jumped back in the lake.

▪ Old Nub Foot ▪

In July 1947, I got Old Nub Foot. He was 13 feet and 6 inches long. His picture was put in the *Chronicle* by Chester Rogers, and also on some postcards. I killed three alligators over 13 feet long that year.

▪ The Lady of the Den ▪

The female 'gator is much sassier than the male, all the way from the time she hatches from her egg. The largest female alligator I ever saw was a 12-footer at Chenango in Brazoria County. She snapped the hook pole off just above the hook, the pole being about 3 inches in diameter.

▪ More About the Beast ▪

The jaws of a 10-foot alligator can be held together with your hand if he don't roll, but when he gets his mouth open, he has plenty of power for closing it. A 'gator is bad about catching things with his mouth and then rolling over and over to wring something loose. If a large 'gator caught hold of a man's hand, he would probably wring the arm off at the shoulder. A 13-foot 'gator will weigh close to double the weight of a 10-footer. Alligators are awfully curious and will go for a mile or two to get past some noise that they wonder about. If you ever find a 'gator in a hole in the marsh and mess with him for a while, he is not likely to still be there when you come back again.

▪ Close Quarters With a 'Gator ▪

A 'gator hunter should always carry a hatchet with him. After shooting a large 'gator, you can grab the 'gator by the nose and lip, hold his head across the stern of the boat, and chop him in the back of the head. Don't just drag him in the boat the first thing or he is likely to come awake and clean the decks. I have had this to happen to me. I shot a 'gator one night in Reds Bayou, about 7 feet long, and just pulled him into the boat. I got my foot on his head and was about to chop him in the neck when all at once he came alive. If I had weighed 2 pounds less he would probably have got hold of me, but I finally got him killed.

▪ The Mating Call ▪

In the spring of the year, alligators over seven feet long beller quite a bit. When water is over the marsh, the female will usually do most of the bellering and the male will crawl as far as a mile in a straight line toward the sound to get in the waterhole with her. When 'gators beller they are vicious-looking sights. They lay in the water and stick their head and tail in the air. But they won't make a sound if they think something or somebody is nearby. The most dangerous place around a 'gator is at his side where he can hit you with his tail. Everything his tail hits goes in his mouth. A 'gator lays in the water with his legs at his side and swims with his tail. You cannot outrun a 'gator for a short distance on dry land.

■ The Hunter's Attitude ■

I have hunted nearly every marsh from High Island to Bay City the past 30 years. I have drawn some blanks, but have also made some good hunts. It is sometimes a hard life and a hot time with that sun beaming down in that high grass and cane. Sometimes it seems you can barely get enough air to breathe. If you are an old man, it will get you quickly.

■ Muskrats ■

In muskrat trapping, 30 to 70 'rats is a fair catch in one night with 140 to 150 traps. 'Rats travel the best when the temperature is around 40 degrees as they like cold weather. There won't be much of a catch in 60 degrees or above. Cold, clear and still nights with temperature about 35 or 40 degrees is perfect. Two 'rats will build a nest, or bed, about 4 or 5 feet in diameter and about 3 feet high in one night out of marsh grass and mud in which to put their young 'rats. If high water stays over the marsh too long it will kill the 'rats out, because they then eat the grass tops instead of the roots. This gives them the bowel trouble. They have to have the roots to live. The best muskrat catch I ever made was 73 'rats out of 95 traps, but this doesn't happen very often. Double-jawed trigger traps are used to catch muskrats so they won't wring out of the trap. After a few years of trapping, a man should get to where he can skin two muskrats per minute.

■ Rabbit Hunting ■

In 1937, Bill and I killed 2,200 swamp rabbits. In October 1936, we got 700 rabbits.

■ Buffalo Seining ■

In 1941, Bill and I seined 8,000 pounds of buffalo fish out of Stephenson Lake.

▪ Ice Fishing ▪

When I was between 12 and 15 years old, I used to push my boat around Cotton Lake when it froze over during the winter, and pick up fish. I would find a hole in the ice and in it would be a fish, numbed from the cold. I would just pick him up, throw him in the boat, and go look for another, until I got a boatload. They were catfish and buffalo. The mud roads were about impassable those days so it was hard to get through with the old Model-T to take the fish to town.

▪ The Big Geese ▪

The big ringneck geese are so gentle over at our camp, you can almost kill them with a sling shot.

▪ Catfish Bait ▪

Earthworm is my favorite bait for catfish in muddy water, and cut mullet in clear water. I used to catch lots of them using about 25 or 30 trotlines, but the past two years they have been very scarce. During spring rises in the river, earthworms have proved to be the very best bait. Wood sawyers are the best in winter for large cats. Most of the time they will bite sawyers when they won't bite anything else. In lakes and overflow water, catfish feed on the top of the water. The closer to the top you can hang your hooks, the better. The catfish comes straight up at the bait, and they smell the bait and sometimes taste it before striking. I have seen the time cats would be biting fresh cut mullet up on the river, but would not touch a bait over 15 minutes old. Most of the time a [gasper] gou fish will taste a bait before taking it and most of the time they never really strike. They make more of a drag like a crab than a strike. The crab is the biggest nuisance the fisherman has for getting the bait off his hooks.

▪ Warm Weather Trapping ▪

We have been trapping mink mostly this winter [1950] and they are scarce this year. So far, we have caught only about 500 muskrats on account of warm weather, and not over 35 or 40 mink. Mink are selling for from $8.00 to $20.00 this season, and muskrats for $1.20, 80¢, 60¢ and 10¢. We have had the worst winter for trapping. The weather is so warm, the 'rats don't come out of their beds. You can find where a 'rat has been coming out a short distance in warm weather and set a trap for him, but he usually won't come back there anymore. But in cold weather, he will come back. The two 'rats build the bed overnight. I don't see how they can do it. They carry the grass in their mouths. A quick rise in the river will drown the small ones. In cold weather, the 'rats will range out from 100 to 200 yards from their bed.

▪ Muskrat Bite ▪

A large muskrat can nearly whack your finger off. In 1927, I was trying to find a lost trap in a 'rat run. I stuck my hand up in the run and a 'rat grabbed my finger. I slung him about 20 feet high and his teeth pulled the meat from my finger. I can still feel the effects of that torn finger sometimes.

▪ Floundering ▪

From 1929 to 1932, money was hard to come by to buy groceries. During the summer, Bill and I waded in the bay, looking for flounder fish to make a living. We camped on Cove Bayou, Dunn Bayou, and Long Island Bayou. We would catch from 10 to 90 flounders a night. Sold most of them for 12¢ a pound. We didn't make much money, but we lived.

▪ From Frogs to 'Gators ▪

I used to hunt bullfrogs for a living part of the year. Once when I had been hunting frogs all night, I heard a big 'gator beller out in the marsh about 3:30 in the morning. The next day I went out in the high seacane in that direction and found a 13-foot bull 'gator and a 9-foot female in the same den.

▪ Polecats ▪

In my school days, I had a trapline through the woods from home to the school house. I would leave early from home so I could run my traps on the way to school. One morning I had five skunks in my traps, and when I got to school, the teacher sent me home because I had too much polecat musk on me. I got $5.00 apiece for some of those polecat skins I caught that day. Not bad for a boy in those days. My dog used to dig polecats out of their holes and when he saw what it was, he would just walk off and leave the 'cat alone. He didn't want to tangle with the polecat.

▪ Musky Observations ▪

I think the musk of a muskrat has a good odor. In fact, some cologne has muskrat musk in it. A mink has a musk that smells more like a cottonmouth moccasin.

▪ More Warm Weather Trapping ▪

We haven't had any cold weather this year [1950] at all. So far it is the warmest winter here in 60 years, since 1890. Yes, it has been bad and warm all winter here at Anahuac and Cove, Texas. In fact, I have several 'gators spotted in the marsh. I think I might start hunting them rather than trapping muskrats. I know of a trapper at Eagle Nest Lake, near West Columbia, Texas, who went out to his 'rat traps one morning and never came back. Lots of big 'gators in that country. They supposed a 'gator got him. They found his boat, but never found him. Hope this doesn't happen to me.

■ Hoopnet Fishing ■

Thinking about fishing, I like to fish with hoopnets better than any other way. When the river is on a rise, the fish come downstream with the current for not more than two minutes. Then they have to turn around and swim back against the current to catch their breath, and then they make some more headway downstream. When they are swimming back upstream, they swim into hoopnets. These nets have throats in them. Most of the time the fish head toward the back of the net and cannot find the center of the hole in the throat to get back out. But if the current changes direction, they will find their way out because the throats of the net will turn back the other way. The fish cannot swim with the current for more than two minutes. I have seen them when they had to get out of a shallow place by swimming with the current in a falling tide. They would still turn around and swim back against the current. I have seen the buffalo fish in such shallow water that they would have to swim on their sides.

■ The Gordy Marsh ■

This marsh I am trapping in now is the Gordy Marsh on Canada's Ranch. It lies north of Lake Surprise and Stephenson Lake. I used to pole hunt 'gators in it back around 1935 or '36, and there were very few muskrats in it then.

■ Seining for Buffalo ■

I also have a buffalo seine 1,200 feet long. During the summer months I have caught some fair catches. The most I ever caught in one haul was 1,600 lbs., and in another, 1,200 lbs., mostly all buffalo fish. Once in three days work with the seine, we pulled in 3,400 pounds of fish by dressed weight. A seine that is hung right will fish good in up to 12 feet of water. It will stand up about five feet between the cork line and lead line and catch most of the buffalo in that spot. The buffalo go to the bottom to try to get out from under the seine and are caught near the lead line. Catfish will swim over the top of the seine. Speckled trout will go to the bottom and can be caught with a 3-foot-wide trammel net. A sudden noise or racket will sometimes cause a complete school of trout to be caught in a net. They will all try to get out under the net and get caught in it.

■ 'Gator Hunting by Hand ■

I went out to run my traps the other day [1950] and forgot to take along my .22 pistol. Wading along in the marsh in about kneedeep water, hunting a place to set a trap, I came across a 'gator's head sticking up right down beside me. There I was, had left my gun at camp. The 'gator was about six feet long. I thought a while and finally decided to try to take him with my pocket knife. I opened the blade of the knife and put it in my carrying jacket. I grabbed his tail to try to raise him up out of the water far enough to reach his head with the knife, but every time I pulled his tail, he would strike at me with his mouth. Finally, I got his head at the top of the water and quickly grabbed him around the jaws. I held his mouth with one hand and stabbed him in the back of the head with the other. He never knew what hit him. I then skinned the 'gator and went on trapping.

■ Buttons ■

Sometimes you get a 10-or 12-foot gator and then find that the hide has "buttons." Buttons are hard bones that sometimes grow in the hide on the belly side of the 'gator and are also called "belly buttons." Large females have them most. A hide with buttons only brings half price.

■ Table Delicacies ■

Alligator meat is fine eating, the meat down the sides of the tail being the best. Muskrat is also good eating, which most people don't know about. They taste something like a squirrel. 'Gator meat tastes something like a large catfish, but is better.

■ Hunting Near East Bay ■

I have just finished four hunts during the past six weeks down in the East Bay marshes. I managed to get 40 'gators from 6 to 11 feet long. I haven't got a 12- or 13-footer yet this year [1950]. Got one 13'-6" and another 13'-8" last year.

■ Cottonmouth! ■

The cottonmouth moccasin snake is the worst enemy the 'gator hunter has. Many times I have been struck at by these large snakes, but so far have been lucky. Cottonmouths are deadly poisonous. Unless a man gets treatment pretty soon after he has been bitten, he might likely die. Many times while trailing 'gators in the marsh, I have run across a large cottonmouth, coiled up in the grass with its mouth wide open and ready to strike. I have waded through marshes where the regular water moccasins and fish snakes were so thick I would have to keep kicking them out of the way to keep from stepping on them, but these snakes won't hurt you. But when you see a stump tailed cottonmouth, you had better not try kicking him around. I have caught a few cottonmouths in my muskrat traps. I have seen these snakes as big around as a man's arm. Once I was pole hunting when the marsh was all dry except for one alligator hole. I walked up to the edge of the pit, looking for 'gator sign, and had approached the den pretty fast. When I stopped and looked around, there were cottonmouths everywhere and I likely had been struck at several times while walking up to the hole, looking for 'gator sign. I got my pistol out and started shooting a trail back through them so I could get out and away from the 'gator hole.

■ The Young Marshman and the Way It Was ■

When I was 12 years old, I was duck hunting. In those days there were very few duck hunters, just a few of the people who lived around here at Cove. I started trapping skunks at that time too, and when I was 14, I started trapping muskrats with single-spring and double-spring Victor traps. That was before they made the two-trigger 'rat trap. I have spent most of my life since then in an outboard motor skiff hunting frogs, 'gators, ducks, 'rats, coons, mink and fish, which turns out to be hard work, but I love it.

■ A Muddy Gun in Matagorda ■

I made another hunting trip for alligators in the swamp near Bay City in Matagorda County. Another friend went along with me for the hunt. The water was almost knee deep over the swamp and we found a hole with two fair-sized 'gators in it. I gave my friend the gun to shoot the 'gators with and I went around behind the hole to find the 'gators underground with the iron rod. About that time, the old 11-foot bull 'gator came out of the hole, but we didn't see him because he was underwater. When the female came out, she stuck her head up and my friend shot her. About that time, the old bull started back toward the hole. We were almost between him and the den. He now had his head on the top of the water and here he came right toward us, not more than 15 feet away, and us in knee deep water and mud. Instead of my friend shooting the 'gator, he threw the gun down in the mud and water and ran up a tree and hollered back at me to get the gun and shoot the 'gator. I stood real still and the old 'gator passed by my leg and went back into the hole. If I had moved, he might have taken my leg off. I finally found the gun and it was full of mud and water. We cleaned the gun up, but was never able to get that bull 'gator out of the hole again. When we got back out of the swamp, my friend never did want to go back alligator hunting with me anymore. I won't tell his name. Ha-ha.

▪ Floating Turf ▪

Back in about 1937, Harley Maley and I began hunting alligators on Mr. Canada's ranch. We hunted the Willow Marsh, which is one of the most dangerous marshes in this country. Lots of floating turf there with no bottom under it. There are some places where you can walk around it, but other places where you fall through. One day I walked out toward it from my boat and all of a sudden the marsh started giving way under my feet. I had to get down on my hands and knees and crawl back to the boat, even sliding on my stomach in some places.

▪ Alligators in the Floating Turf ▪

There was an open pond of water in the middle of the floating turf in the Willow Marsh, about 50 yards wide and 150 yards long. Harley and I dragged a little boat to it one night and saw a bunch of 'gator eyes shining. We broke some stalks of seacane and put them in the boat with us. Then, we started pushing up to the 'gators and shooting them with the rifle. Each time we shot one, we would stick a cane down by him where he sank, and go to the next one. We killed 13 big alligators in that pond that night and then went back to the canes and pulled the 'gators into the boat and took them to shore. We did it that way so we wouldn't scare the rest of the 'gators off by loading the first one in the boat, because they make a lot of racket, spinning around and flopping their tails when you load them, and will scare some of the others back to their dens.

▪ Crabbing ▪

I have about 85 crab traps and last year I ran about 65 of them every day. My traps are made out of wooden slats. The traps are about three feet long and about two feet wide at the bottom, and about ten or twelve inches at the top, sort of like a triangle. The opening at the top is about twelve inches long and just wide enough for a crab to get through flatways. The bait is tied to the bottom of the trap with a wire, and bricks in the bottom of the trap holds it down in the water. I like to keep my crab traps in about six to eight feet of water and run them every morning during the summer. I have a line of crab traps about two miles long in Trinity Bay. In five months of crabbing, I missed running them only three days on account of bad weather.

▪ A Neighbor Named George King ▪

Back in about 1919, there was an old man named George King who moved into the old Jane Wilburn house across the gully in the woods on the north side of Cotton Lake. He was an old fisherman and trapper and was deaf, but we got along pretty well. He claimed to be a brother of the man who ran the King Ranch– at least this is what he said. But he wanted to live on the river and fish for catfish for a living, although his folks kept after him to live a different kind of life. He was around Anahuac during the late 1800's, and lived on Jack's Pass where it entered the river, and sometimes on Southwest Pass. He was at Jack's Pass when the 1915 hurricane came, and was washed out to the highland on a big log. He rode on one end of the log and an alligator on the other end. They both washed ashore on Mayes Island near Wallisville.

■ The Trinity River Passes ■

In December of 1926, I camped part of the winter on Cove Island, which is one of the oldest known hunting and camping grounds for settlers around Cove. It was in the best hunting and fishing area in this part of the country and was a place goose hunters used to camp the night before rowing the remaining four miles or so to Southwest Pass, where they went goose hunting for the early flights of snow geese. Southwest Pass had several deep prongs running into the bay and was once believed to be the mouth of the Trinity River itself, and around the small deep passes were sand bars which the snow geese came to. They still come there even though the passes are all filled up now. Back north of Triangle Pass is a place called Jack's Pocket.

■ Rabbit Hunting in a Strong Norther ■

Cove Island is on Cove Bayou, about 300 yards from the bayou's mouth at the bay. The bayou used to be very shallow at its mouth with oyster reefs, but has been dredged out the past few years for an oil drilling rig to get into it. One night while camped on Cove Island in 1924, when Guy Maley and I were coon trapping, it blew in a hard blowing norther from the northwest. We decided to go rabbit hunting with our headlights. We took our boat away out in the bay so the tide wouldn't leave it aground while we were hunting. At dark we started hunting swamp rabbits. By 10 o'clock we had 100 rabbits. We carried the rabbits out to the boat and found that the strong north winds had blown the water out farther than we had thought it would, and left our boat aground on the sand. After loading the rabbits in the boat, we walked back to the bay's shore and found some posts to pry the boat out to the water. The water was so low, we had to go through Southwest Pass to try to get into the river so we could head for home. We spent the rest of the night tugging the boat on the sand, trying to find the mouth of the pass. Oh, what a night that was. We finally got home and hauled our 100 rabbits to the market in Houston where we got about 30 cents a pair for them. That don't seem like much money these days, but it was big money back then.

▪ Bay Bottom Floundering ▪

The sandy bay bottom between Cross Bayou and Cove Bayou used to be the best floundering grounds around here. I caught many flounders along this stretch back in the 1930's and '40's. Used to gig from 20 to 30 flounders a night along there.

▪ More Buffalo Seining ▪

About the year 1942, my brother and I owned a buffalo seine together. We had seined buffalo fish from the mud lakes around Cove for years. It was made of 3-inch-square mesh net, which gave it a 6-inch-stretch mesh. We caught tons of buffalo and gar. We knocked some of the gar in the head and threw them back, because they eat so many other fish. It is said that the alligator gar can eat his weight in fish every day. We fleshed and skinned the buffalo and shipped them by express to St. Louis, Missouri and New York, all iced down. We received anywhere from 2¢ to 8¢ or 10¢ a pound, according to the size.

While alligator hunting on Stephenson Lake, we found there were also big buffalo in the lake. This inland lake is about two miles long and about 3/4 of a mile wide and was fresh water at the time. Mr. Canada owned the land around the lake. He is a very nice fellow and he allowed us to seine the lake. We got about 8,000 pounds of buffalo after a few days hauling. One evening we went to the north bank of the lake to make a drag for some carp that stayed in that end of the lake.

▪ Hunting in a Blue Norther ▪

About the year 1916 or '17, duck hunters used to come from Houston and drive out here [to Cove] over the mud roads from Cedar Bayou. We lived in a big two-story house at Cove. Papa or Bill or me would row the hunters across Cotton Lake and into Wet Marsh Pond, which is all closed water nowadays to everybody except members of the Potlikker Hunting Club.

One warm day in January, three men came to go duck hunting. We sometimes got as much as $3.00 a party to row them to the hunting marsh, which was a lot of money in those days. Ed Hill, one of my old hunting buddies, stayed all night with me the night before. Papa and my older brother, Bill, were gone when the three hunters got to our place, so Ed and I said we would row them across the lake for their hunt.

Ed and I were barefooted, as usual. We walked with the hunters across a strip of marsh about quarter of a mile wide between Cotton Lake and Wet Marsh Pond. The pond is about a half mile long, north and south, then turns and runs about a mile and a half west toward the Lawrence woods.

After we had been shooting ducks a while, it popped out a bad norther, a real blizzard, and the temperature went to freezing, it seemed all at once. By 8:30, I could not cock my gun, my fingers were so numb. I started walking to warm up, and in about an hour went to look for one of the men who had walked farther back in the marsh. I found him lying down by a big pile of ducks on a string he had killed. He had dozed off to sleep and I figured he would be frozen there if I left him alone. So I poked and shook him and kicked him with my bare feet until I got him to notice me. Then I got him up and carried his gun and ducks and he hung onto my shoulder as we walked back toward the boat at the lake. As he bogged along in the pond, he began to thaw out some. When we got to the boat, we found Ed and one of the other hunters walking around in circles to keep from freezing, but one of the men was still missing. We didn't have any idea where in the marsh to look for him. The other hunter said he thought the missing man had caught a ride out of the marsh with another bunch of hunters, which I thought must have been George Wilburn's hunters. We turned the boat up on its side a while on the lakeshore to knock the wind off of us, but then decided we had better get the half frozen man back home if we could. I didn't want to leave without the other man, but his friend said again that he had gone in with some other hunters. So we started back across the lake against the hard-blowing north wind. Hundreds of ducks were flying and swirling low over the lake everywhere in the wind and it was really something to see.

I rowed the boat for about an hour, barely making any headway against the wind. The other hunter, who was a big man, put his hands just above mine on the oars and started helping me row. Ed and the other cold man were now groaning and about frozen out, when at about 3 o'clock in the evening we saw Papa and Uncle Eli Hill, Ed's daddy, coming out in another skiff to meet us.

When we finally got back home, Ed and the cold man were just about out of their heads from the cold. Papa had a big fire blazing in the fireplace and they had to hold the cold man back as he tried to crawl into the fire. Ed was as blue as he could be. When the cold man went to leave Cove and head back for town, he said to Papa, "Well, Mr. Clark, the next time I go duck hunting, it will be on a hot day in the middle of July."

▪ Odds & Ends on Kills & Catches ▪

In a month between May and June in 1929, I killed 228 alligators. – In October 1936, Bill and I killed and sold 700 swamp rabbits for about 30¢ apiece. – On the 10th of October 1937, we killed 206 rabbits which sold for from 20¢ to 35¢ each. – Winter of 1934-35, I caught 1,316 muskrats; winter of 1935-36, I caught only 536 'rats; in 1936-37, only caught 350. – Year of 1927, I killed 139 alligators. – From 1920 to 1937, shipped over 1,000 'gator hides to market. – Year of 1933-34, caught about 600 muskrats and 19 mink. – Winter of 1931-32, I killed about 1,000 ducks. – Winter of 1937-38, caught 727 muskrats. – During seven days in March 1939, I caught 3,300 pounds of buffalo fish. I caught 432 muskrats in winter of 1939-40. – Had an early frost in 1939 and started rabbit hunting on October 9. – I saw a goose over Wet Marsh Pond on June 17, 1940. – I caught two muskrats in one trap on January 5, 1939. A storm killed all the rabbits in the marsh in 1941. – Captured a 12-foot alligator alive in 1928. – Bill and I killed 42 'gators one night in 1941. – Caught between 10 and 12 thousand pounds of buffalo fish in October 1941. – From May 15 to June 15, 1942, caught 8,500 pounds of buffalo in Lake White. – From June 15 to July 30, 1942, caught 1,100 dozen crabs; caught 200 dozen of them in one day. – July 5-15, 1943, caught 2,700 pounds of buffalo in White Lake. – In May 1943, got 32 alligators in Cross Bayou in five nights. – In winter of 1945-46, I caught 3,129 muskrats. – Got 17 'gators in Bastrop Bayou in 1946. – About the same time, got a 13-foot alligator in Cane Pond and a 13 1/2-footer out of East Gum Bayou, off Lost River. Sold the big one for $28.50. – Our camphouse burned on December 4, 1950. It burned again in 1954. – In 1946-47, caught 3,400 muskrats. – I would guess I have killed a total of somewhere over 3,500 alligators. – Summer of 1951, killed only about 50 'gators. – Bought my first crab traps in 1957. – Saw 57 snow geese flying in one bunch on May 24, 1958, which is late for them around here. – In 1958, Bill, Vane and I caught over 3,600 nutria; over 1,000 of them were large size. – In February 1959, sold 93 large nutria in New York for $2.46 apiece. – More catfish this year [1959] than in the past few years; have caught several thousand pounds on trotlines. – One day in 1921, I killed 40 ducks, all big ones, no teal, at Big Pond with a single-barrel gun and 33 shells. – One night I killed 25 rabbits with 25 shells while standing still on a log down near Garden Bayou. – Caught two nutria in one trap on a night in 1968.

▪ New Hunting Partners ▪

My boy is getting old enough now [1954] to go out alligator hunting with me. I punched a seven-footer out of the hole the other day, but instead of coming up at the mouth of the tunnel, the 'gator stuck his head up at the edge of the pit, right where my boy Kendon was standing with the rifle. Poked its head up almost right between his feet. But Kendon made a dead shot on him. He said, "Daddy, I didn't know at first whether to shoot or run." I told him it wouldn't have been very wise to run, because the movement of his feet would have given the 'gator an open sideswipe at his leg, but if you stand still, the 'gator won't strike. But he will bite anything that moves. I took Kendon and my nephew James Howard Hoffman, Jr. with me on a hunt again a few days ago. I let Kendon punch the 'gator out of the hole while I shot this one. The 'gator didn't bother the boys – neither did the boys bother the 'gator.

■ Weather Notes ■

Cotton Lake froze over from January 19th till the 27th, 1942. It snowed four inches on the 22nd of January, 1940. Storm came September 23, 1941, and washed my net house away. Our camp house was washed away in Hurricane "Carla" in September 1961. On January 28, 1951, a strong norther came in at 4:00 in the evening and by Monday, the 29th, was freezing hard. Temperature from Monday to Saturday stayed between 12 and 32 degrees. Temperature was still 17 degrees that Saturday morning even though the wind had gone around to the south. 1949 storm filled my boat landing with logs and drift. Worked 30 days to get it cleaned out. It was 50 degrees on May 23, 1967. One day in mid-July, 1967, the temperature dropped to 56 degrees. The hurricane in August of 1915 was the worst one here since the big storm of 1875, they say. In the 1941 storm, Cliff Rosenquest rode the storm out in 12 feet of water in a willow tree at Jack's Pass. His only company was a big coon. His houseboat was washed away. The 1915 storm was the worst one in my life so far. Had a 26-degree freeze on March 27, 1955. From August 28 till October 24, 1958, tidewater stayed 16 inches deep over most of the marsh. Big rise on the river killed nearly all the muskrats in the spring of 1920. We had a big snow, about 6 inches deep, in February 1960. 1949 storm brought a 12-foot tide; so did 1959 storm ["Debra"]. In 1961, "Carla" brought us 15 feet of tidewater.

■ A Lot of Ducks, But Small Limit ■

The duck season of 1961 was the best one here in the past 12 or 15 years, because there were so many ducks. But the law would only let you kill three ducks a day, so not many hunters turned out. I don't know where the people who decide on the duck limits get their reports, but they must have got a false one this year. Everybody hereabouts know there were more ducks here than for many years.

■ Hurricane "Carla" ■

Hurricane "Carla" came along September 11-12-13, 1961, and wiped out many lowland houses in which we lost our trapping camp of two buildings in the marsh on Wilborn's Ranch, near Robinson Lake below Double Bayou. We trapped muskrats there for over 20 years, but the nutria had about taken over the place during the past several years. We caught many thousands of them over there. "Carla's" tide got every bit as high as the water in the 1915 hurricane. I caught some large catfish after the storm on trotlines and their tails were all bruised from being banged around by the logs and drift washed against the hillside north of Cotton Lake and Old River Lake. Big logs blown in by the storm killed alligators by beating them to death against the banks. The string of drift and logs, anywhere from 50 to 100 yards wide, stretched for miles along the hillside. Under the drift were hundreds of dead turtles and thousands of dead nutria. Chairs, beds, butane tanks, and parts of houses all washed up here from Smith Point and Bolivar Peninsula, being blown across Trinity Bay. But we never found anything of our camp house. Thousands and thousands of nutria were dead in the drift, but they will be back again if we don't keep them down by trapping them. Cottonmouth moccasins were everywhere in the drift and were all mad at being washed out of the marsh and were ready to bite anything that moved. Everything that lived in the marshlands was blown against the highland. During the big storm, our marshes were nothing but an ocean of water about 15 feet deep.

▪ Reflections ▪

Well, it just looks like there is no use in trying to make a living any longer shrimping in the shrimp season. I now go out and drag and tear up my nets, not making any money. Also, the muskrats were very scarce last winter.

No fishing this spring on account of water conditions. My hoopnets are all tarred and ready to set out, but looks like I will miss this spring run altogether. And not many 'gators to hunt anymore. It just looks like it is about all over. But after doing this kind of work for a living all my life, I remember there have been other times when things looked like we couldn't make it like this any longer; then something would turn up for the better. I will go out and try again.

I would love to see a time again like it was back in 1931, when I was on a lake alligator hunting in a small boat, 30 inches wide and eleven feet long. When the 'gators were so thick I counted 25 of them in one little corner of the lake. I would load my little boat down with 'gators, haul them to the bank, unload them, and go back to shine more 'gator eyes with my headlight. Then, the next day was spent in skinning the 'gators and salting down the hides.

Then, looking back a few years, when I dumped several bushels of big shrimp on the deck of my shrimpboat and lowered the trawl to make another drag. Crabs and small fish all had to be culled out of the shrimp and cast back overboard before they died.

And a few years ago, when I hauled a thousand to twelve hundred pounds of buffalo fish in with my 1,200-foot seine. Sometimes my helphands and I would have to knock as many as 500 pounds of garfish in the head, trying to get them loose from the seine.

And those days it was nothing to catch between 50 and 150 pounds of catfish on the trotlines on the runs twice a day. I usually baited with earthworms and ran about 700 hooks twice a day. I spent nearly half my life time digging for earthworms to bait the lines.

And then, I can look back years ago when I might run as many as 160 muskrat traps a day and catch from 40 to 80 'rats on a good cold morning. But I guess those days are over now. There are more people in the marsh than animals and birds. We even see people down there now who we don't even know. All they want to do is shoot their guns and make a lot of noise. But I guess that is the time we are now living in. I don't see how it can get much worse, but I guess it can.

• APPENDIX A •

THE PIPE

Throughout history, men have been associated with various objects by which they are often identified by the public or those who know them best. Henry Ford had his automobile; General Robert E. Lee had his horse, "Traveler." Who can view the distinctive design of the swastika emblazoned across the center of a flag without visions of Adolph Hitler? And among the legendary tales of the Old West, who can dare imagine the Lone Ranger without his mask, silver bullets, white stallion named "Silver," and his "faithful Indian companion, Tonto"? The latter, without these pieces of equipment and his redskin sidekick, might never have thrilled audiences through the decades as "the daring and resourceful masked rider of the plains."

In a more local sense, Cove folks have come to associate Manson Clark with his tobacco pipe. While he did not smoke a pipe in his days of youth, he did display in other ways the propensity of the young Southern male for the use of tobacco. For many years, as a young man, he rolled cigarettes of the popular Bull Durham tobacco, poured into the paper from the familiar white pouch with the drawstring. When rolling cigarettes became too time consuming (there were no handy factory-packaged "ready-rolled" brands then), he turned more and more to chewing tobacco. His favorite brand was Day's Work, a popular plug type chew, but after a few years he began to develop severe sieges of heartburn from its extensive use. Due to this condition, he finally gave up the chewing tobacco. Through his years of working the marshes, he never completely lost the craving for a good chew now and then, and in later life would again indulge in the juicy tobacco leaf, but on a much more limited basis.

At the time of his turning from chewing tobacco, during the 1920's, he decided to try pipe smoking. The first few days of this venture with his new pipe almost set his mouth on fire, as is common with the novice who enters this realm of the tobacco world. But, in no time he became accustomed to the hot smoke from the pipe tobacco – and somewhat of a trademark was established. Wherever Manson appeared, there also was the pipe. In the early days of Manson and the pipe, his brand of tobacco was Prince Albert, but he later changed to the Half and Half brand which he maintained the remainder of his life.

More important than the tobacco, however, became the pipe itself. It mattered little whether or not the tobacco was smoldering or, indeed, even if there was any tobacco in the bowl of the pipe. Just so the pipe itself was in his mouth – that was what really mattered. Although he rarely removed the pipe from his lips except when sleeping, eating or attending church, it usually did not burn the tobacco for more than three or four hours daily.

The bowl of a pipe has the tendency to build up the ashen residue from the tobacco alongside its inner walls to a point that it almost becomes as hard as the wooden bowl itself. While a younger breed of pipe smokers are wont to scrape this buildup of burnt ash from inside the bowls of their pipes, many of the oldtime smokers scorn such a practice. The gradual buildup of the residue inside the bowl actually causes the pipe to smoke cooler, and it might take a pipe smoker several years to form the proper thickness of the burnt, hardened ash inside the bowl so that the pipe will be exactly to his liking. Often, after years of extensive use, the bowl of one of these veteran pipe smokers will hold only a small pinch of tobacco and that must sometimes be packed down into the bowl with a matchstick, the largest object which will fit into the center of the bowl between the seasoned walls of hardened ash.

Charley Roberts was such a veteran of the pipe. For a classic example of the dire importance of the precise buildup of ash inside an oldtime smoker's pipe bowl, we look to one of Charley's excursions to the mudflats of lower Old River, near Lawrence Island, southeast of Old River Lake. The area was one of the fisherman's favorite "hauls" for seining for buffalo fish. On this day, Charley fed the seine overboard to the desired length and then went into the shallow water with the net. Placing his pipe on a wooden boat seat, he departed the vessel to begin the swath with the seine. While he was thus employed, his friend, J. C. "Seaf" Wilburn came to the haul from Lawrence Island to see if Charley was having any luck. While waiting for the fisherman to complete the haul, Seaf noticed Charley's pipe on the boat seat, the bowl caked almost shut from years of tobacco use. In what would normally be considered a good deed, Seaf took out his pocket knife and began to chip and scrape the seasoned residue from inside the bowl. By the time Charley finished his haul and returned to the boat, Seaf had completed his work and replaced the pipe on the seat, confident that Charley would approve of the new condition of his pipe. As Charley waded back to the boat, he greeted Seaf in a cordial manner. Then, he spotted his pipe. Taking the pipe between his fingers, he turned it around several times in his hand, carefully studying its new features. Showing little emotion, Charley said, "Humpf. Ruined my pipe." He then tossed the pipe into the muddy waters of Old River and went about his business of fishing.

Of the several Gospel evangelists who have traveled to Cove to conduct Gospel meetings of a week or two weeks duration at the Church of Christ since its beginning in 1908, none was better loved by the congregation than Alva Johnson of Turkey, Texas. As is always common when a visiting preacher is in a rural area conducting a meeting at the local church, various members of the church are eager to invite the evangelist to a meal or two at their homes during his stay. Manson always looked forward to Brother Johnson's meetings, not only because of his dynamic preaching, but the two men had something in common – their smoking pipes – and they never failed to tease each other about how they planned to continue working until they finally were able to "convert" their pipes.

During the slashing winds and torrential rains of Hurricanes "Debra" and "Carla" in 1959 and 1961, respectively, Manson worked out in the violent elements at his boat landing, attempting to rescue boats and other equipment. His pipe was held firmly between his teeth to avoid the valued instrument from being blown from his mouth. Since he obviously could not expect to keep a fire of tobacco smoldering within the bowl in such weather, the pipe was turned upside down to keep the bowl from filling up with rain water.

It has been stated by some that the use of tobacco is a form of Southern patriotism, that in the use of the southern grown leaves, the user performs his part in stimulating the economy of the South. If such reasoning indeed be the case, Southern economists must find great relief in the stoic form of Manson Clark and his pipe.

■ APPENDIX B ■

THE FUR BUYERS

Everything done by the fur trapper on his trapline and in his hidehouse is geared toward one special day – that occasion when the fur buyer inspects the trapper's pelts for the market. During the grading of the furs by the prospective buyer, thoughts of all other matters are left outside and strict attention is paid to the manner in which the buyer deals with and for the furs. Quite often, the buyer and the trapper are longtime friends, their business associations spanning years or decades, but during the grading process their relationship is all business. The buyer naturally hopes to obtain the trapper's furs at as reasonable a price as possible so that he might receive a profit at a later date, but still pay the trapper enough for his furs in order that he might buy from him in the future. On the other side of the coin, the trapper realizes that the buyer must make a profit in order to remain in business and is willing to allow him to do so – within reason.

After the furs have been graded, the pelts are counted in each grade and arranged in neat stacks of ten skins each. The buyer then pulls a pad and pencil from his pocket and begins figuring the overall price he will offer the trapper for his wares. Shortly, the buyer will look up from his figures and quote to the trapper the amount his furs will bring. If the trapper considers the sum to be reasonable, he will nod his approval. However, if he honestly feels his catch is worth more than the amount offered, the operation of the free enterprise system is put to the test, and often strained to near limits as buyer and trapper joust for dealing positions. A casual passerby outside the furhouse might never guess that the two men inside are friends as he hears the trapper exclaim, "Now, what's the matter with this hide? It's a top quality 'rat if there ever was one!", to which the buyer might retort, "The fur's too thin on the bottom. That's a good price for what you have!" The dueling might continue for some time on either the grade on a few, specific pelts or the overall price and grade of the lot.

Regardless of the outcome of the sparring match inside the furhouse, tranquil relations return following the fray. The men often sit down together over cups of coffee and discuss the fur market or other matters relating to the business.

Manson Clark dealt with practically every fur buyer in southeast Texas at one time or other, as well as with marketing houses throughout the nation. When the market is tight on the local front, furs are often securely wrapped, tagged and shipped to distant markets. He shipped furs to Funsten in St. Louis, Missouri, Taylor Fur Company in Louisville, Kentucky, United Fur Brokers in New York City, New York, and numerous buyers in such scattered locations as Houma, New Iberia, and New Orleans, Louisiana, Griffin, Georgia, and Cedar Rapids, Iowa. However, the greatest number of his furs throughout his long outdoor career, were sold locally. Unless there is a great deal of difference in the price of furs being offered locally and elsewhere, the trapper has to take into consideration the cost of freight charges in shipping the bulky cargo to distant markets.

Not many people are aware today that Sears-Roebuck & Company was once a major national fur buying outlet in the days when its business was primarily engaged in the mail order trade. As such the huge company found itself on both ends of the fur industry, both in purchasing raw furs from American trappers and selling the finished products to the fur-wearing public.

In Goose Creek (now Baytown), across Cedar Bayou in Harris County, Jack Heard bought furs from numerous local trappers. Operating from his large buy-sell-and-trade store just off Main Street, Heard dealt in a large volume of raw furs during each winter season.

The fur buying business is similar to the stock market in many ways, and fur buyers come and go on a fairly routine basis. It often takes a shrewd business mind to know when to buy and sell, especially in large volume. A rule-of-thumb is that a fur buyer should never sink more money into the purchase of fur than he can afford to lose as the fur market is extremely erratic, fluctuating daily throughout the year, but especially during the heavy fur trading seasons. Countless are the number of buyers who entered the fur business at what appeared to be a promising time in the market, only to be financially wiped out after one season's fling.

Some regional fur buyers have managed to weather the economic onslaughts and stay with the business as a lifetime trade. Two of these with whom Manson Clark and other Cove area trappers dealt for decades were Ed J. Rosenquest of Smith Point and J. H. Welborn of Beaumont.

Ed Rosenquest operated his fur business at his home on the Point for many years. A talkative and very likeable man, he bought most of the muskrat furs trapped by Manson and the other trappers on the Canada and Wilborn ranches during the 1940's and '50's. Trappers recall him as a man who would "rear and charge" over the slightest discrepancy in his fur grading from one of the trappers, but the trappers remember Mr. Rosenquest as one of the best fur graders in the business. During the 1950's, as the nutria began to make their inroads in the marshes, Manson and his brother, Bill, decided to pull a trick on the veteran fur buyer. One of them caught a small nutria, about the size of a large muskrat, but totally worthless in value on the market. They skinned the animal, stretched the hide over a muskrat wire, dried the pelt, and slipped it into the next bundle of muskrat furs they took to Smith Point. They were confident that everyone would join in a great round of laughter when Ed came to the nutria skin and attempted to grade it as he would a muskrat. When the long awaited moment came, they did all have a good laugh, all that is, except Ed Rosenquest. Flinging the pelt aside, he launched into a verbal diatribe against the trappers, believing that they had actually tried to pass off a worthless article before his well trained eye.

Rosenquest once lost a large investment in mink furs when at a peak in the market prices he had bought heavily. As the fur market is so apt to react, the bottom fell out of the mink market practically overnight, and Ed was left with an enormous stockpile of mink and the choice of whether to increase his expenses with the cost of cold storage or sell the furs at the greatly reduced price. Ed Rosenquest had a home in Florida, where he resided much of the time, but still came back to Smith Point for extended periods. Well known and liked among the inhabitants of the small fishing village on the Point, his return trips from Florida were always heralded by area trappers asking the question, "Is he going to buy fur this winter?"

J. H. Welborn, longtime Beaumont businessman, was one of the most familiar figures on the fur buying circuit in southeast Texas. In his eighties, Mr. Welborn was not as able to make the rounds of fur buying as he once was, but continued to send his agents on the circuit to the fur houses of the trappers. Welborn and his buyers had been coming to Cove since the 1930's, visiting in the homes of the trapper families and grading their furs in their fur houses. Acquiring quite close relationships with a number of the area families, he came to be recognized variously by the nicknames of "Shorty" or "Pappy." Like Ed Rosenquest, "Shorty" Welborn acquired a reputation among trappers of the region for giving the trappers a good grade on their furs.

During the 1970's, Mr. Welborn and his wife underwent a severe beating inside their Beaumont home by a pair of hoodlums, and would-be robbers, who had forced their way into the house with the intention of taking the money he kept for the buying of furs. When the couple refused to reveal where the money was hidden, the thugs inflicted a merciless beating upon the elderly man and his wife. This terrible experience did not stop Shorty from buying furs, but it did teach him to no longer keep his fur money at home.

The entrance of the nutria into the American fur market during the 1960's stimulated the market for southeast Texas trappers for several years. It brought back into the buying circuit such oldtime buyers as Chester Myers of Beaumont. Also entering the buying market at intervals were some new faces: Gene Dutton, Larry Wilburn and Chuck Peting of Cove, and Steve Wilburn of Barbers Hill.

History has indicated that success in the fur buying business depends largely upon the individual buyer's willingness to give the trapper a fair grade for his catch. The trapper has put in many long, hard hours in securing his animals on the trapline and preparing the furs for the market. He keeps a watchful eye on the trends in the market and has a good idea of what is happening in the big fur brokerage houses in New York City. He usually has more than one fur buyer in mind when the time comes to offer his furs for sale and the buyer knows that the seasoned trapper knows as much about the grade of furs as any fur dealer. (Manson had numerous buyers offer to allow him to grade his own furs during prospective sales.) The buyer who most consistently delivers the best grade on the furs will be the buyer who purchases the greatest number of furs and is most likely to remain in business the longest.

THE MONEY MACHINE

The Great Depression of the 1930's had been a long, drawn out period of tight finances for practically everyone, but toward the end of the decade matters had begun to ease to a degree. The fur and hide markets showed definite signs of strengthening and it looked like things were going to be all right after all.

In 1938, Manson and Bill heard a bit of news that caught their fancy. It seemed that a man in Baton Rouge, Louisiana had perfected the ultimate instrument for locating buried treasure. All you had to do was pass the contraption along the surface of the ground and when it crossed a spot where the treasure was located, a buzzing in a set of earphones would indicate exactly where to begin digging to recover the gold, or silver, or whatever it happened to be. The price for the whole outfit was $150.00. That was quite a large sum of money with fringes of the Depression still lingering and an entire generation of Americans having learned from the past few years that to be frugal is to eat.

With all the tales that had always floated around Cove about buried gold both on the highland and in the marshes, most of it supposedly planted by the men of Jean Lafitte's pirate band more than a century ago, they should have little trouble finding someone else who would be interested in buying into such a venture. They talked to George H. Schaeffer and his son, Lawrence, and found them willing to enter into the investment with them.

The elder Mr. Schaeffer decided to stay home while the younger men made the trip to Baton Rouge to survey the object of their intentions. So Bill, Manson and Lawrence packed a few belongings into Bill's car and headed eastward for Louisiana. Bill had just recently put new rings into the engine of his car and after such a delicate bit of mechanical surgery the vehicle could not be driven at high speed. They made the entire trip to Baton Rouge at a top speed of some thirty miles per hour. The final leg of their journey, crossing the Mississippi River on a ferryboat at the edge of the city, must have seemed quite speedy after their slow trek from Cove.

After asking directions a few times from local citizens, they finally pulled up before the home of G. O. Maher, inventor, manufacturer and seller of the famed "Money Machine." Invited into his home, they were given a demonstration of how the machine operated. Compared to the metal detectors of a later day, this contraption was a monstrosity. It consisted of two wooden detector rings, each more than two feet in diameter and wrapped with black electrical tape. The rings were held some three feet apart by a wooden "A"-frame of sorts in the center of which was fashioned a handle for balanced carrying over the area to be surveyed. A wooden box contained upwards of four of the old crank telephone type batteries of cylindrical shape. The box was equipped with a leather strap to facilitate the hanging of the heavy encumbrance about one's shoulder. Earphones were included and could be adjusted on the operator's head much like a pair of cold weather earmuffs. The entire conglomeration was connected together by a series of electrical wires, complete with plugs and outlets.

The Cove men paid Maher the $150.00, broke the machine down into five parts so that it would fit into Bill's car, and found themselves a room in the city for the night. Early the next morning they left Baton Rouge, re-crossed the ferry on the Mississippi River and headed back home with their merchandise.

Back at Cove, Mr. Schaeffer was content to allow his son and the two Clarks to scour the woods and marshes for suspected caches of treasure, confident that if something were discovered he would receive his rightful share on his investment. After a few such ventures into the field, Bill tired of the fruitless searches. Urged on by the buzzing of the detector, he had helped dig a number of two-to three-foot-deep holes in the earth, which was about the maximum depth the machine would pick up a signal from metal, only to find a collection of old nails or plow points. It had not taken them long to realize that the machine reacted not only to gold or silver, but also to almost any other such mineral in the ground.

Manson and Lawrence kept searching, however, for some ten years or more whenever Manson could break away from his trapping or fishing for a few days, and when Lawrence did not have to be at work in the family rice fields. They soon became accustomed to the idea that they were not apt to locate any treasure and merely reconciled themselves to digging up artifacts and relics from old homeplaces in the area. They would often dig into the earth at a particularly "hot spot," especially on one of the numerous marsh islands, only to find that the detector had reacted to a liquid iron ore deposit in the ground.

All sorts of metal objects were discovered during the course of a number of years, but not so much as a penny's worth of meaningful "treasure" was ever unearthed by the searchers and their "money machine." Once asked why he did not spend more time at the helm of the machine, Manson answered, "A man would starve his family to death trying to make a living with that thing."

▪ APPENDIX D ▪

THE FEDERAL STING

(Author's Note: At the discretion of the writer, the following was not included in the original edition of this work in 1983, although the occurrence had taken place almost three decades prior to that date. Though Manson felt it might be a good opportunity for him to relate in detail exactly what had happened on this occasion, I, in charge of compiling the text, chose to omit the account. My reasoning was twofold: (1) Federal authorities are not above retaliation against those who reveal in any way the sometimes questionable tactics of their operations; (2) At the time of publication, Manson was seventy-seven years of age, not in the best of health, and should not have been subjected to any such action should it have been forthcoming. The following is a synopsis of the events of the previously omitted experience. – K.L.C.)

In the opening days of the 1955-56 waterfowl hunting season, the annual ritual of catering to the city folks in their quest for feathered prey on Cotton Lake began anew. There were the regulars, many of whom had patronized Clark's Duck Hunting for years and, in a few cases, for decades. Mingled among them were a number of new faces who were testing their skills on the lake for the first time as well as a few who had never fired a load of shot at a winged target in their lives. A small number of the latter category would join the ranks of the "regulars" and become steadfast customers while the greater portion would soon grow weary of fighting the sometimes uncomfortable elements on the lake or become discouraged upon the realization that not every hunt would produce a legal day's limit of ducks. One of these new faces belonged to an individual who claimed to be a wristwatch salesman named Anthony "Tony" Stefano.

Coming to Cove from Houston, as did the majority of Manson's customers, Stefano appeared to be an enthusiastic hunter, although he never appeared to have much luck in his pursuit of the fowl. Usually among the early arrivals on the mornings of his scheduled hunts, he would share the pots of coffee Myra kept brewing for the arriving hunters prior to the departure for the lake. After returning from his hunt, he never missed the opportunity to stop back by the house for more coffee and maybe a slice of cake before heading back to Houston. Not appearing to be disheartened by his inability to bag a number of ducks, it appeared that Tony was on his way to being one of the frequent hunters on Cotton Lake.

After several sojourns to Cove in which he appeared to take note when Manson also occupied one of the blinds on the lake for a brief hunt, he began fretting on his post-hunt stops at the house about not having killed anything. Once, Manson offered him a couple of ducks he had killed that morning. Tony then brightened and offered to pay him for the fowl, but Manson would have none of it. When Stefano refused to take the ducks without paying for them, Manson (ironically, as it would turn out) informed him of the law which prohibited the sale or purchase of wild waterfowl. Tony went back to Houston empty-handed.

After a couple more hunts in which Tony persisted in trying to buy ducks from Manson, he made what proved to be one final hunt on Cotton Lake. Drawing a blank for his efforts, Stefano stopped by the Clark home again and virtually begged Manson to sell him some ducks. He claimed to have invited some friends to his Houston home the next day and had promised them a duck dinner. Manson thought it odd that anyone possessed of such bad luck in the field of hunting would make such a commitment, but he nevertheless felt sorry for the now almost frantic figure before him. He presented Tony with two bluebills, the only ducks he had managed to bring in that morning. Stefano again started to pull some bills from his wallet, but Manson told him to put the money away or he would take the ducks back. Tony then said he needed more than two ducks with which to feed his friends and asked if Manson knew anyone else locally who might have more ducks he could obtain. Manson told him that his brother-in-law, Harley Maley, who lived on the hillside overlooking Manson's boat landing, had gone hunting that morning and might be in a position to give him a couple more.

Hurrying back down the little road, Tony caught Harley outside at his shop in the process of cleaning some ducks he had killed that morning. Harley was glad to see Stefano as he wanted to tell him that a wristwatch he had recently purchased from him had already quit running, and needed to learn whether or not he could receive a replacement. Tony told him they would talk about that later, but that he was now in a hurry to get back to Houston. He asked Harley about relieving him of two of the ducks he had as yet not finished cleaning. Noting the man's apparent desperation, Harley handed him a couple green-winged teal ducks. Stefano instantly produced two one-dollar bills in return. Harley told him, "No, I don't want that," and stepped back from Stefano. Tony then reached forward and stuffed the bills into Harley's shirt pocket. Without another word, Stefano abruptly wheeled around and hurriedly got back into his car, and left.

In April 1956, Federal warrants were served on more than fifty men along the Texas coast. Charges ran the gamut of various infractions of Federal laws relating to the commercial trade in waterfowl. Manson and Harley were among those netted in the operation. Both felt there had to be some sort of error in their cases until the name of Tony Stefano was interjected into the proceedings. Harley was charged with the outright sale of the two teal he had attempted to give the undercover agent while Manson 's charge was for "conspiracy" to sell ducks since the previous fall he had suggested that Stefano check with Harley who might give him a couple more ducks.

Although Manson and Harley were among the "smaller fish" netted in the sting operation, they both felt they had been "out-foxed by the fox," and any effort to fight the charges before a jury would be a long and drawn-out ordeal. Both entered pleas of nolo contendre, or "no contest," indicating they were not pleading guilty to the charges as specified, but were waiving any opportunity to take their cases further. They paid fines and were given two years of probation during which time they were not allowed to hunt waterfowl. Manson was permitted to continue operating his hunting guide business during the probationary period.

▪ POSTCRIPT ▪

LINZIE GRIFFITH

Earlier in this study Linzie Griffith of Cove is mentioned in the text in present tense as being among the Cove area trappers of many years who come together at times for discussions of past trapping experiences. Since the completion of the text, Mr. Griffith has passed from this life and a word is considered in order here to bring the earlier reference up to date.

Sam Linzie Griffith was born December 9, 1901, to Charlie and Laura Elvina (Tilton) Griffith. His birthplace was his lifelong home of Cove. A descendant of the pioneer Griffith, Barrow, Tilton and Hartman families of the region, Linzie was another of those men who made his livelihood from the fruits of nature, much as his frontier ancestors had done. Variously engaged in farming, fishing, hunting and fur trapping, he, too, had many tales to relate of his experiences. Always willing to tell others of past days, his jovial and congenial manner drew listeners to his side on a regular basis.

He worked for many years as caretaker and guide for the Chambers County Hunting Club (Potlikker Club) in the marshes south of Cotton Lake. An avid muskrat trapper, he was extremely regretful to see the introduction and upsurge of the nutria in the area marshes and adopted the nickname of "bench-leg" in reference to the short-legged rodents.

He was recognized among most Cove area trappers as perhaps the best otter trapper in the region. During his latter days, he was troubled continuously by physical imbalance and at least once a fall incapacitated him for a lengthy period. Still, when the trapping season rolled around, he would often be seen running a few traps along the banks of Old River. The trapping blood ran freely in the veins of Linzie Griffith.

Mr. Griffith passed away on December 7, 1982, just two days prior to his eighty-first birthday.

▪ PHOTOGRAPHS ▪

The following several pages feature a variety of photographs relating to aspects of the work performed by the Marshmen of Cove during this century.

■　■　■　■　■　■　■

In 1948, Chester Rogers compiled a collection of photographs he had taken of Manson Clark at his work in the marshes and presented them to Clark in a black leatherette folder. Inside the front cover of the collection the photographer entered these words

"This little volume of
fine photographs is dedicated to
MANSON L. CLARK
a hunter of deadly aim who lives
with earnest honesty,
in the opinion of the compiler,
C. ROGERS."

5-28-48

BILL CLARK, MANSON CLARK AND HARLEY MALEY
At Their Trapping Camp in Canada Ranch Marshlands
PHOTO BY CHESTER ROGERS

HARLEY MALEY
With a Nice Catch of Flounder
Trinity Bay – 1947
PHOTO BY CHESTER ROGERS

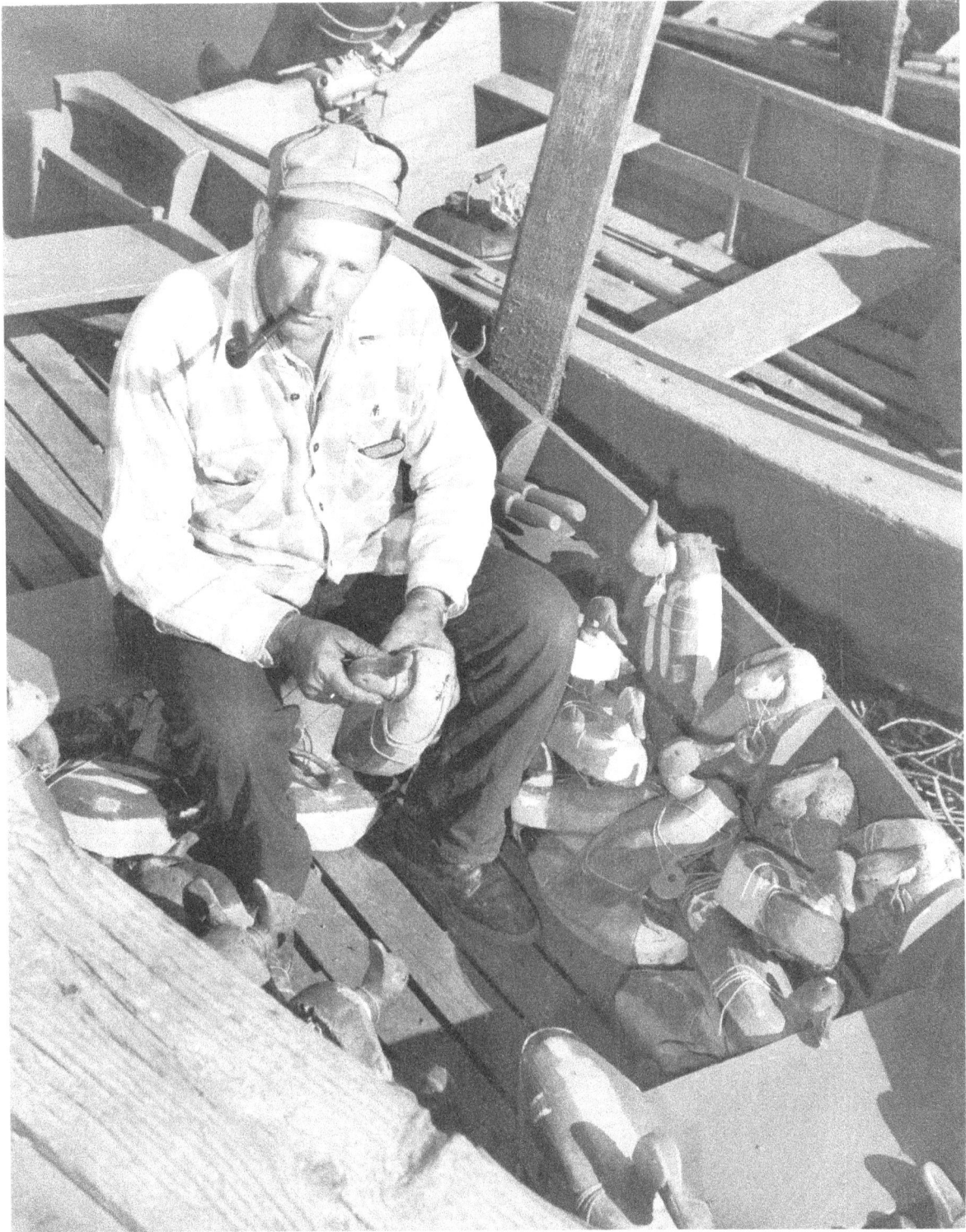

MANSON CLARK
Preparing for Next Morning's Hunt
Clark's Boat Landing, Cove, Texas
PHOTO BY CHESTER ROGERS

139

MANSON CLARK TAKES AIM ON "OLD NUB FOOT" – JULY 1947
Alligator's Eyes Protruding from Water Just Below Point of Forked Log

CLARK REMOVING THE TOUGH HIDE FROM "OLD NUB FOOT"
PHOTOS BY CHESTER ROGERS

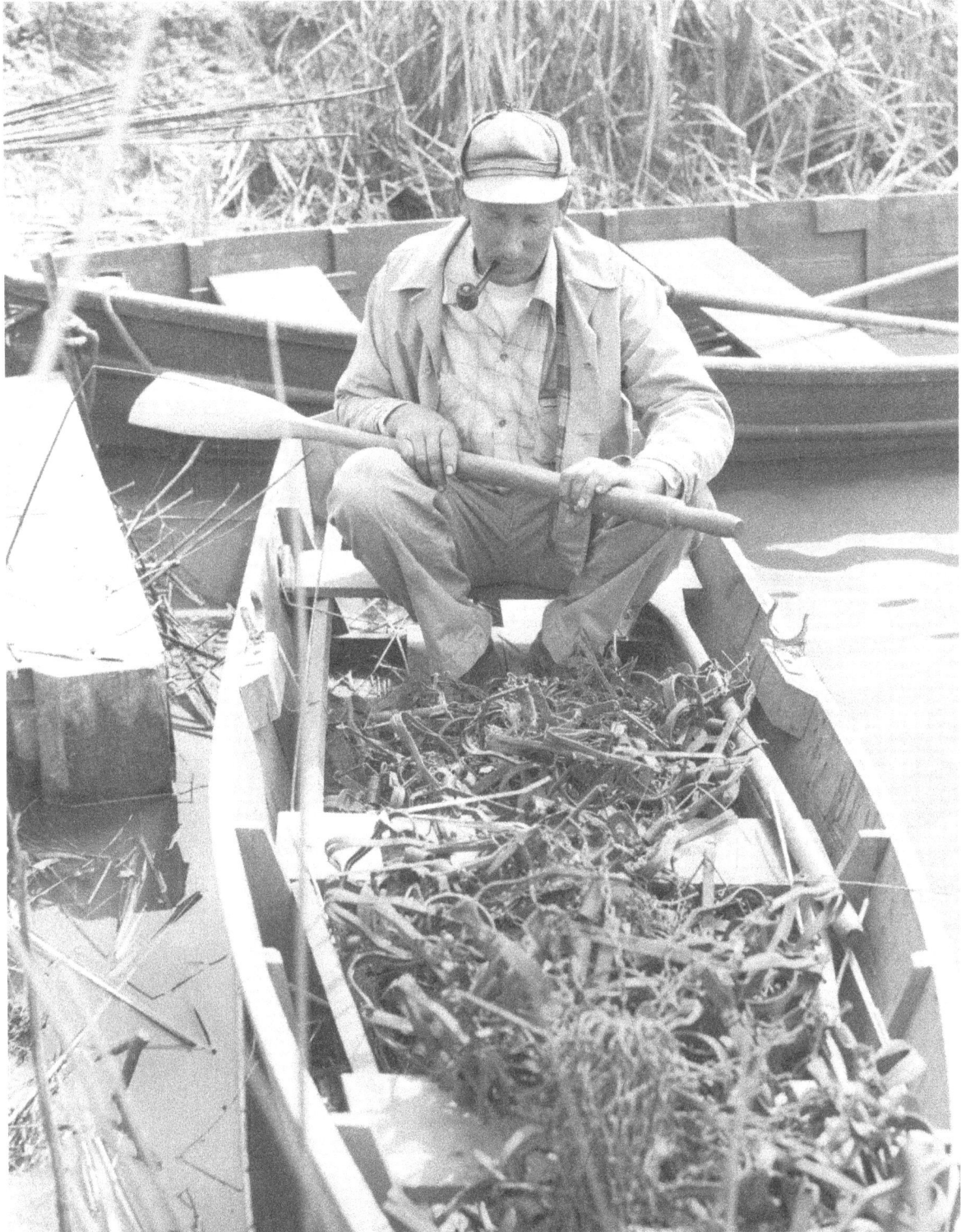

MANSON CLARK AND BOATLOAD OF MUSKRAT TRAPS Departing for the
Trap1ine -December 1947 Canada Ranch Marshlands, Chambers County, Texas

PHOTO BY CHESTER ROGERS

BILL CLARK EXAMINES MUSKRAT PELTS

MANSON CLARK AND PERHAPS THE FIRST NUTRIA
EVER TRAPPED IN CHAMBERS COUNTY -1950
PHOTOS BY CHESTER ROGERS

WELCOMING THE *"FREDA"* TO COVE
Some of the Residents of Cove Who Gathered on the Banks of Old River in 1950 for
the Arrival of the *"Freda."* Pictured are some who went aboard for a Trial Run.

CLARK'S HUNTING BOATS docked at his
new Boat Landing at the Joe Maley Place in
Cove in 1947

CLARK'S BOATS moored on the North
Shore of Cotton Lake in 1960.

MANSON CLARK ON NUTRIA TRAPLINE
PHOTO BY LARRY CAWLEY, SILSBEE, TEXAS

Cross Bayou in Cove, Texas Marshes February 28, 1979

Clad in two hooded coats and other heavy winter gear, Manson turns his back to a chilling north wind as he paddles his boat along the west bank of Cross Bayou, checking nutria sets. At age 73 at the time this photograph was taken, he had converted in recent years from a wooden trapping skiff to an aluminum boat, the first such craft he had ever used in his work that was not built by either his own hands or those of another local trapper or fisherman.

Having suffered a severe stroke a scant four years prior to this scene, he was hospitalized for an extended period of time. Determined not to miss a winter on the trapline, he worked diligently (sometimes stubbornly) in rebuilding his strength during the following summer. The month of November saw him heading back into the marshlands with a load of traps.

BILL CLARK and Son STUART
inspecting a Muskrat Bed in Lawrence
Marsh – 1935

CATFISH (mostly MUDCATS)
on Manson's Fish Rack at
his Boat Landing.
The Boys are (L to R) Kendon Clark
and Jamie Hoffman,
Manson's Son and Nephew – 1949

GEORGE WILBURN BLIND
With Decoys, in Eastern Sector
of Cotton Lake.
One of about 20 Blinds maintained
by Manson on the Lake – 1948

MANSON
Working his Furs at
Houseboat-turned-Hidehouse in 1972.
Nutria pelts in Yard, Muskrat
pelts hanging on Wall.

145

MANSON CLARK fleshing hide of "Old Nub Foot" while son Kendon looks on.
July 1947

SOUTHEAST TEXAS

Upper Gulf Coast Region

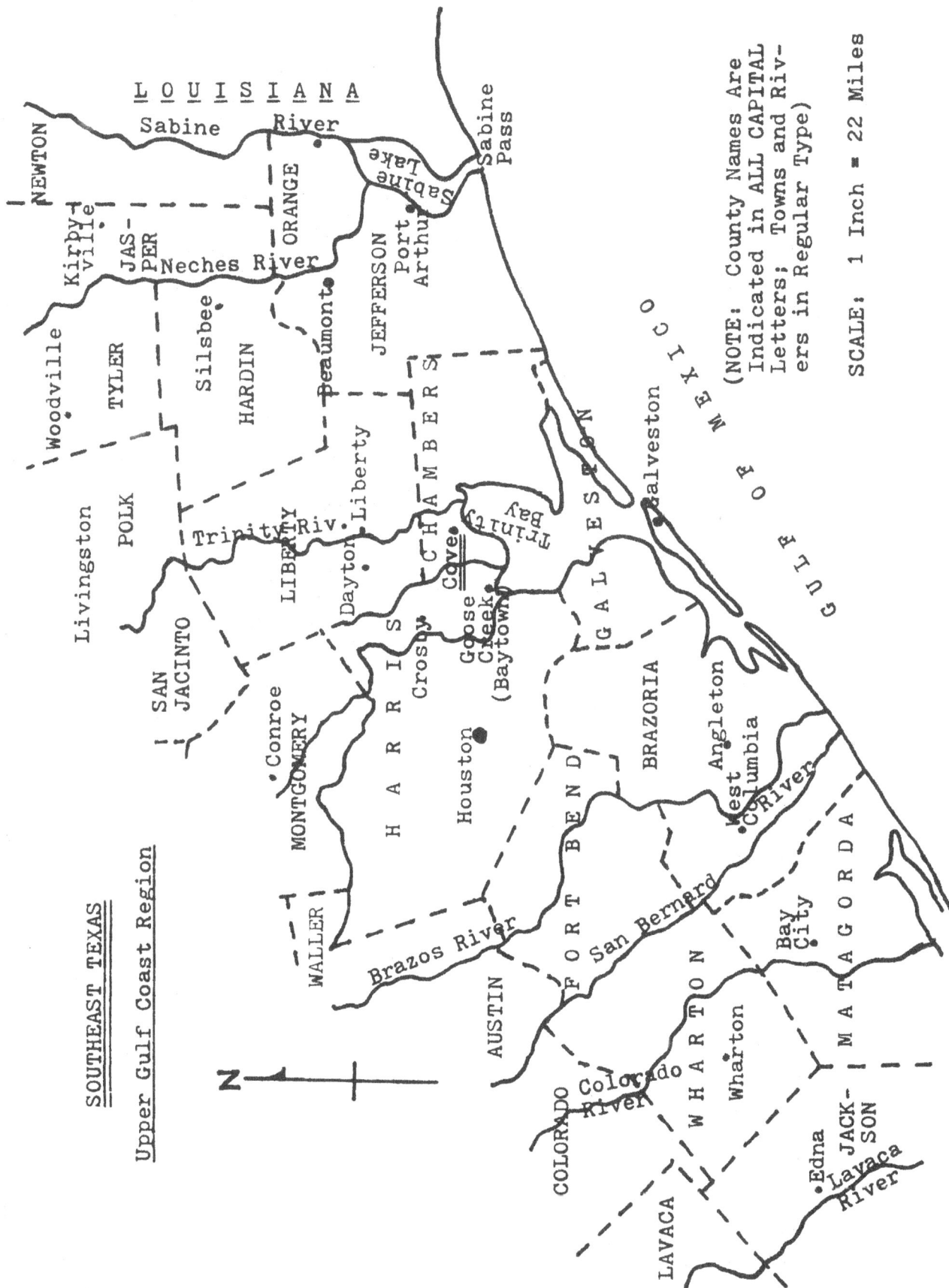

L O U I S I A N A

Sabine River

NEWTON

Kirby-ville

JASPER

ORANGE

Sabine Lake

Sabine Pass

Neches River

Port Arthur

JEFFERSON

Beaumont

Woodville

TYLER

Silsbee

HARDIN

Livingston

POLK

Trinity Riv.

LIBERTY

Dayton

Liberty

CHAMBERS

Trinity Bay

SAN JACINTO

Conroe

MONTGOMERY

Crosby

Cove

Goose Creek (Baytown)

HARRIS

Houston

GALVESTON

Galveston

GULF OF MEXICO

WALLER

Brazos River

FORT BEND

San Bernard

BRAZORIA

West Columbia

Angleton

C.River

AUSTIN

Colorado River

COLORADO

WHARTON

Wharton

Bay City

MATAGORDA

LAVACA

Edna

JACK-SON

Lavaca River

N

(NOTE: County Names Are Indicated in ALL CAPITAL Letters; Towns and Rivers in Regular Type)

SCALE: 1 Inch = 22 Miles

147

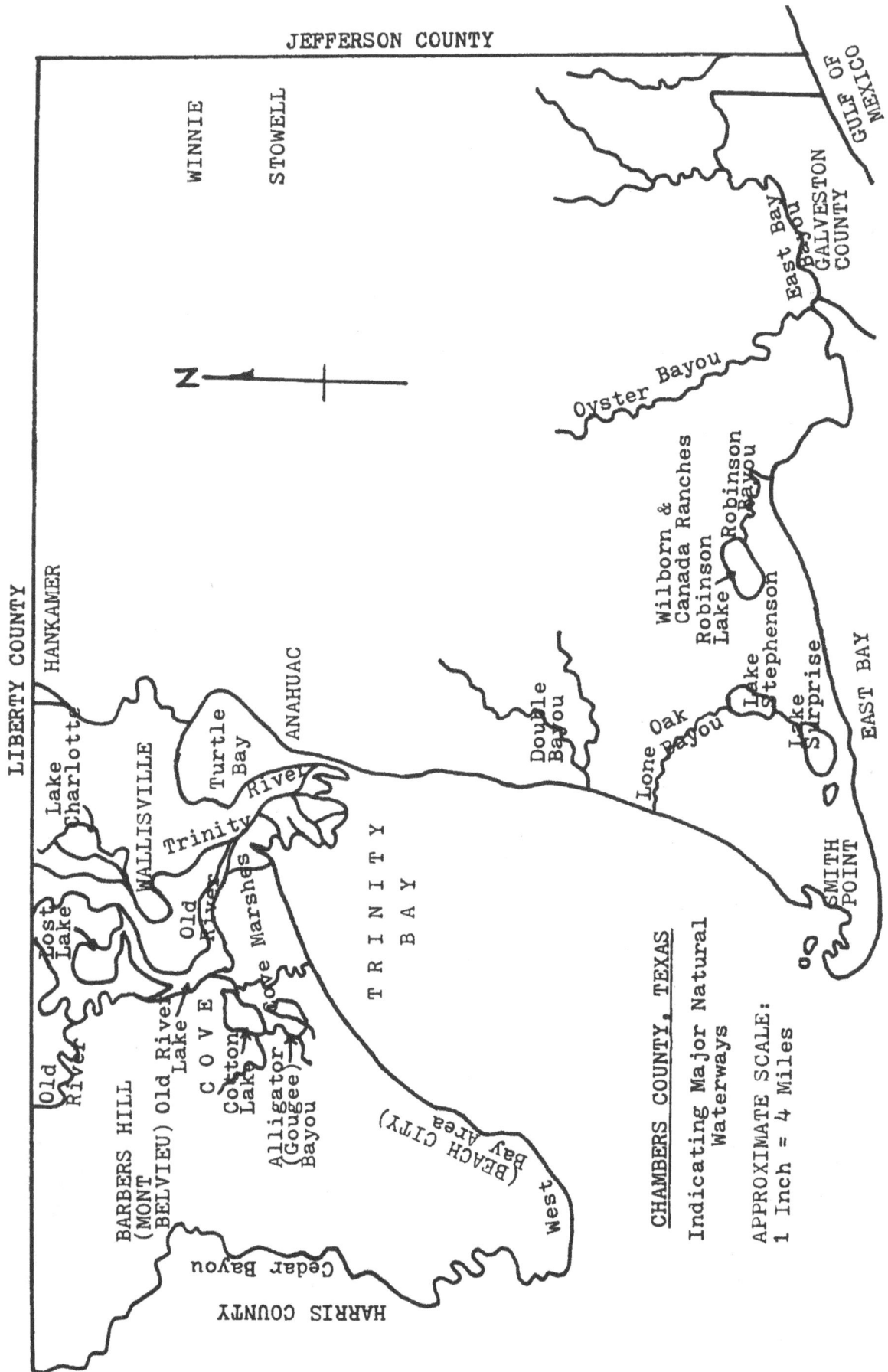

JEFFERSON COUNTY

GULF OF MEXICO

WINNIE

STOWELL

GALVESTON COUNTY

East Bay Bayou

East Bay

Oyster Bayou

Robinson Bayou

Wilborn & Canada Ranches

Robinson Lake

N

LIBERTY COUNTY

HANKAMER

Lake Charlotte

WALLISVILLE

Turtle Bay

ANAHUAC

Trinity River

Old River

Cove Marshes

T R I N I T Y   B A Y

Double Bayou

Lone Oak Bayou

Lake Stephenson

Lake Surprise

EAST BAY

SMITH POINT

Old River

Lost Lake

BARBERS HILL (MONT BELVIEU)

Old River Lake

Cotton Lake

Alligator (Gougee) Bayou

COVE

West Bay Area (BEACH CITY)

Cedar Bayou

HARRIS COUNTY

CHAMBERS COUNTY, TEXAS

Indicating Major Natural Waterways

APPROXIMATE SCALE:
1 Inch = 4 Miles

▪ EPILOGUE ▪

Manson Clark had reluctantly accepted a form of semi-retirement during the early 1980's. Following several bouts with a chronic heart condition which landed him in a hospital several times, he first gave up his fishing. To him, the act of fishing did not mean merely sitting in a boat with a hook or two dangling in the water. Rather, it meant staying on the water for several hours at a time, running and baiting trotlines consisting of hundreds of hooks.

He had even given up duck hunting as a complete waste of time. As the number of firearms-toting people pouring into the marshes increased, so proportionately did the quality of the hunters decrease until Manson was no longer willing to put up with their antics. He merely made an occasional trip through the marshes to view what was going on as somewhat of a source of amusement.

There was, however, one form of his outdoor life he would not relinquish. Each November, Manson would be seen heading back into the marshlands to begin another season of fur trapping. He might pull his traps out of the marshes for three or four days per month during the winter – just long enough to acquire some much needed rest – but was soon back on the trapline in quest of the nutria, coon, mink and otter.

The winter of 1985-86 was Manson's final trapping season. Having observed his eightieth birthday on November 28, 1985, he trapped the marshes hard during the next three months. Occasionally leaving his boat at the bank of a bayou for a mile-long walk across a boggy expanse of marsh, with a sack of traps across his shoulder all the way, younger men would see him slowly making his way across the muddy terrain and later ask him how he did it. "Slow and steady," was his usual reply. "Never get in a hurry in the marsh, or it will kill you." Therein lay a lifetime of advice for others who might heed the call of the marshlands in later generations.

On August 6, 1986, Manson was feeling fine. Although he had had another severe round with his heart while picking dewberries in a field in Cove on an unseasonably hot day the previous spring, he had had the rest of the spring and most of the summer to recuperate. In this hottest month of the year, he was already making plans for the coming winter's trapping season.

In the mid-morning hours of that day, he had just returned home from a walk to Cotton Lake, and was sitting on the porch swing at his home, attempting to cool off from the day's heat. Suddenly feeling quite ill, he stood, went into the living room, sat down in his chair, and turned on a small electric fan on a nearby table. Gripped by a massive heart attack, he passed from this life almost immediately. His daughter-in-law, Mrs. Genie Clark, who lived nearby and was a certified Emergency Medical Technician, was called and immediately began efforts to revive him. Soon, two other Cove medical personnel, Jack White and Jean Peting, arrived with the community's volunteer ambulance service. Manson was rushed to Humana Hospital in Baytown, but all efforts to revive him were in vain.

Two days later, on August 8, graveside services were held in the private family cemetery near his home. Manson Lee Clark was laid to final rest on the family property where he had lived his entire life, and no more than one hundred yards from where he had been born eighty years earlier.

THE BAYTOWN SUN
August 7, 1986

Services set for well-known Cove resident

COVE — Graveside services for well-known fur trapper Manson Lee Clark, 80, are scheduled for 10 a.m. Friday at Clark Family Cemetery.

Leroy Stevens, former mayor of Cove, will officiate.

A lifetime resident of Cove and member of a pioneer Chambers County family, Clark died Wednesday at his home.

Clark hunted and trapped alligators, muskrats, nutria rats, otters, rabbits, squirrels, ducks and other wildlife.

His son, Kendon Clark, wrote a book, "Marshman," which chronicles Manson Clark's hunting and trapping experiences. The book, published in 1983, is based on Manson Clark's journals. The book also includes Clark's ancestry and his childhood memories, as told to Kendon Clark.

"He never got away from the marsh. He loved it," said Kendon Clark of his father. He said his father worked the entire 1985-86 trapping season and was planning for the 1986-87 season.

"He always said he'd never be able to just sit around and do nothing," said the son. "We're thankful he never had to do that."

In addition to his own hunting and trapping, Manson Clark for some 52 years guided duck hunters on Cotton Lake.

A Houston television program, "The Eyes of Texas," featured Clark in 1975.

Clark was a member of Hood's Texas Brigade Association and belonged to the Church of Christ.

THE PROGRESS
August 13, 1986

Area Deaths

Manson Lee Clark

COVE— Graveside services for Manson Lee Clark, 80, of Cove were held 10 a.m. Friday, August 8 at Clark Family Cemetery in Cove with Leroy Stevens, former mayor of Cove, officiating.

Clark died at his home on Wednesday.

A lifetime resident of Cove and member of a pioneer Chambers County family, Clark made his livelihood by hunting and trapping alligators, muskrats, nutria rats, otters, rabbits, squirrels, ducks and other wildlife.

An award-winning feature story written by his son, Kendon Clark, appeared in The Progress, November 18, 1981, telling the story of Manson's fight with Old Nub, a 1,000 year old alligator.

Clark is survived by his widow, Myra Clark; son, Kendon of Cove; daughters, Mrs. Warner (Gloria) Ellis, and Mrs. Kenneth (Freda) Campbell, both of Cove; a brother, Vane Clark of Cove; a sister, Vera Harold of Crosby, eleven grandchildren, eleven great grandchildren and numerous nieces and nephews.

Pallbearers were Alva Clark, Gene Dutton, Ronnie Maley, Jack White, Freeman McKay, and Jackie Griffis. Honorary pallbearers were Manson Clark's many friends.

Anahuac, Texas   THE PROGRESS   Wednesday, August 13, 1986

Arabella Says..

By Villamae Williams

She has so much to tell you she really doesn't know where to start. The really first most important thing is that she has lost one of her best friends. Manson Clark, the Great Marshman, who trapped and hunted in the Cove marshes all his life, gathered up his traps and went away last week. He was buried in a beautiful shady glen near his home, his very favorite place in the whole world, and near his family — his wife and children and other relatives.

But do not be too sad. He had lived a very long and productive life, and he left a legacy which is safe in the hands of his son, Kendon. Kendon has been recording the history of the Cove area through the eyes of his father for many years, and you can be sure another account of early history will be forthcoming, partly due to Manson's love of the land and its people.

▪ INDEX ▪

King Philip's War, 1
King Ranch, 114
KPRC Television Station, 101, 102
KRAJKA, Rudolph, 90, 91, 92
KTRH Radio Transmitter Station, 70
Ku Klux Klan, 34

www.ingramcontent.com/pod-product-compliance
Lightning Source LLC
Chambersburg PA
CBHW062016090426
42811CB00005B/867